ODD GIRL OUT

DOCTOR WITHIN

DR. REMINA PANJWANI

TESTIMONIALS

Dr. Remina Panjwani is more than her impressive title of Doctor of Medicine, she is the embodiment of resilience, grace, and purpose. The modern-day version of The Little Engine That Could, she has overcome countless obstacles along her path. When others said, "You're not good enough…not smart enough…not talented enough…you don't fit the mold," she didn't just prove them wrong, she rose above with quiet strength and unshakable determination.

What makes Dr. Remina truly remarkable is that her success is not measured solely by accolades or credentials, but by the compassion she brings to every patient, the empowerment she inspires in others, and her holistic, integrative approach to healing. She bridges science with soul, treating not only the body, but the mind and spirit as well.

Oh yea, she also happens to be a rockstar speaker, woman empowerment advocate, and a devoted mom of two boys. "Odd Girl Out, Doctor Within" is not just a book about health and wellness, it is chock full of pearls of wisdom, and a powerful reminder of what the human spirit can accomplish when one's fire is lit from deep within!

- Greg Reid **#1 Best-Selling Author,** Founder of **Secret Knock**

Dr. Remina'a story is a powerful testimony of resilience, courage, and purpose. From being told she wasn't enough, to proving—again and again—that she was more than capable. Her journey is one of breaking cycles and rewriting destiny. What struck me most is how she transformed pain into pillars of empowerment, reminding us that education, authenticity, and self-care are true equalizers.

This book is more than a memoir—it's a roadmap to possibility. Dr. Remina invites us to see that the very obstacles meant to defeat us can, with faith and focus, become steppingstones toward our calling. Her voice is both fierce and compassionate, her wisdom practical and profound.

If you have ever doubted yourself, felt the weight of cultural or generational expectations, or questioned whether you can rise above the noise, this book will meet you exactly where you are and lift you higher. It is a gift of courage, reminding each of us: **why not you, and not now?**

- **Dr. Victoria Rader,** Award winning Speaker, Author, Creator and Quantum Personal Development Pioneer, Founder of YU2SHINE

Dr. Remina's story is a tenderhearted testament to resilience, leaving the reader in tears of resonance and hope.

- **Nita Patel,** Artist, Author, Psychologist

Dr. Remina Panjwani's story is one of extraordinary courage, consciousness, and conviction. In her book, she reveals what it means to rise above cultural and generational conditioning and to rewrite your narrative through purpose and self-mastery. Her journey from adversity to achievement—and struggle to self-realization—is not only inspiring, but also instructive. Dr. Remina embodies the essence of leadership: to heal oneself so deeply that your very presence becomes a catalyst for others to do the same. This book is both a mirror and amp for anyone ready to transform pain into power and live in full alignment with who they are meant to be."

- **Richard Dolan** Performance Philosopher, Founder of RICH World, Advisor to Leaders in Business, Sport and Life

Odd Girl Out, Doctor Within

Dr. Remina Panjwani

Copyright © 2025

All rights reserved.

ISBN: 978-1-968149-05-5

Joint Venture Publishing

The Millionaire Mentor, Inc.

All rights reserved. No part of this book may be copied, reprinted, or reproduced in any way, electronic or otherwise, without written permission from the author and/or publisher.

This book is a memoir. It reflects the author's present recollections of experiences over time. Some characteristics might have been changed, some events might have been compressed, and some dialogue might have been omitted or recreated based on memory. Neither the author nor the publisher accepts any liability for inaccuracies or misrepresentations.

No warranties or guarantees are expressed or implied by the inclusion of the content herein. Neither the publisher nor the author shall be liable for any physical, psychological, emotional, financial, or commercial damages.

Photos by Jasmine Jain.

Printed in the United States of America

DR. REMINA PANJWANI

TABLE OF CONTENTS

Testimonials

Dedication

Foreword By Amberly Lago

Introduction

Chapter 1	"Odd Girl Out"
Chapter 2	"Link By Link"
Chapter 3	"The War Zone"
Chapter 4	"I'm Possible"
Chapter 5	"Education: The Equalizer"
Chapter 6	"Pillars"
Chapter 7	"Authenticity"
Chapter 8	"A Holistic Approach"
Chapter 9	"Neuroplasticity & Rewiring"
Chapter 10	"On Purpose"
Chapter 11	"Why Not?"
Chapter 12	"Imagine"

Empowerment Tools

About The Author

MEDICAL DISCLAIMER

The information presented in this book is for **educational and inspirational purposes only.** It is **not intended as a substitute for professional medical advice, diagnosis, or treatment.** Always seek the guidance of your physician or other qualified healthcare provider with any questions you may have regarding your health, medical condition, or treatment options. Never disregard or delay seeking professional advice because of something you have read in this book. The author and publisher disclaim any liability arising directly or indirectly from the use or application of any information contained herein.

DR. REMINA PANJWANI

DEDICATION

This book is dedicated to my boys, Zayyan and Zayden, the loves of my life. Thank you for reminding me daily what the true meaning of unconditional love is. You both inspire me to live life with an open mind and open heart. Your reflection of youthfulness and innocence brings me perspective and joy. I love you more than words can say.

Sincerely,

Mom

FOREWORD

Have you ever felt sick and tired of being sick and tired? Stuck in a rut, weighed down by the past, or wondering if you were made for something more? Maybe you've lived through trauma, struggled with your identity, or questioned your worth. Maybe you're just searching for the energy, clarity, and courage to rise to your next level.

If so—you're in the right place.

You're holding a book that's more than a story. It's a lifeline, a blueprint, a bold reminder that healing is possible, change is real, and you are capable of more than you've imagined.

And the woman behind these pages? She's not just a doctor—she's a warrior of wisdom and a healer of hearts. She's a light, a living, breathing example of what it means to turn pain into purpose and fear into fuel.

Her name is Dr. Remina Panjwani, and I'm honored to call her a friend, and a true inspiration.

Through these pages, Dr. Remina Panjwani invites us into the raw, unfiltered truth of her journey—from being a young girl told she wasn't smart enough, pretty enough, or good enough, to becoming a confident, compassionate, purpose-driven physician, speaker, mother, and mentor.

BShe takes us through the battles of cultural expectations, generational trauma, anxiety, and self-doubt—and shows us exactly how she overcame them, not just to survive, but to shine!

She's done the heavy lifting through life experience, education, service, soul work, and now she's gifting you with the pillars that helped her reclaim her power. Pillar by pillar, page by page, she offers you the tools to do the same.

This book will awaken something within you. It will challenge you to reflect, reset, and rise! Most of all, it will remind you that even when life feels impossible, you have the power to shift to **I'm possible!**

Dr. Remina Panjwani isn't just writing words—she's rewriting rules. So keep reading. Let her story light a fire in you. Let her courage give you strength, and let this book be your permission slip to rise, rebuild, while reclaiming the life you were always meant to live!

Amberly Lago

USA Today Bestselling Author, TEDx Speaker, Podcast Host, Coach

INTRODUCTION

From the outside, her story might look like a straight line of success, a military veteran turned doctor, speaker, and healer. But beneath that polished surface lies the real journey of Dr. Remina Panjwani: the story of a once timid, awkward girl who felt like the "odd girl out." Born to South Asian immigrant parents and raised within the weight of generational trauma and cultural expectations, she grew up in the shadow of "shoulds" and "musts." She was taught to stay small, to be quiet, to follow the path laid before her. But even then, something inside her refused to dim.

Her rise was not born from ease but from endurance. Each chapter of her life, from her childhood battles with identity and belonging, to the rigid halls of tradition, to the fire of military service—shaped her resilience. What began as confusion and conflict evolved into clarity and conviction. She learned to transmute pain into purpose, silence into strength, and expectation into empowerment. Along the way, she discovered that true healing, both for herself and for others, requires more than medicine. It demands compassion, balance, and the courage to integrate both science and soul.

Today as a Doctor of Internal Medicine and a holistic healer, she stands as proof that it's possible to bridge worlds—the analytical and the intuitive, the ancient and the modern, the disciplined and the deeply human. Her approach to care embodies a harmony few are willing to pursue: blending evidence-based practice with integrative alternatives that honor the body, mind, and spirit as one. She is not only a physician, but also a warrior of wellness, a mother whose heart shines through every act of service, and a voice for those who have been told they are too small, too different, or too broken to rise.

"Odd Girl Out, Doctor Within" written by Dr. Remina Panjwani has a simple but powerful message: If I can do it, so can you! Because the truth is, strength isn't measured by size or circumstance, it's measured by spirit. And though she may be small in stature, her heart, purpose, and presence are nothing short of mighty and miraculous. This is her story, of breaking barriers, redefining what's possible, and proving that every "odd girl out" carries within her the power to heal, to lead, and to light the way for others.

CHAPTER 1

"Odd Girl Out"

"You aren't good enough." "You look different." "College is for smart people." These words burned, leaving their mark as if they'd been branded into my soul.

As I look back at my youth, I was burdened by a constant reminder that I never felt good enough. I certainly didn't seem to fit in, even within my own family. Like most children from immigrant families, I knew I was different from the other kids at school and in the neighborhood, but I didn't feel like I belonged anywhere, even at home. Subcultures and communities usually offer a sense of belonging within their own group, and although some of that existed, for the most part I was ostracized for not being pretty, thin, or smart enough. I remember aching over these damaging words and constraints that were carelessly thrown at me.

My psyche was naturally affected. Like any young child who's exposed to conditional trauma, whether it be verbal or physical,—it can be damaging throughout their lives. I heard such horrible things as,

"You'll never amount to anything," or "You aren't good enough." Coupled with the overall thought process of surviving paycheck to paycheck, the cultural subservience of women, and acceptance of mediocrity, my childhood was wrought with conflicting and confusing moments. These limiting boundaries were being put in place for me at such an impressionable age that it's easy to understand how a vicious cycle can carry on from generation to generation—that is, until someone recognizes it and deconstructs it, thus breaking the chain!

I battled with generational, cultural, traditional and parental trauma from a very young age. Words are so powerful that they should not be spoken carelessly, especially to a young person who's developing their brain with the information they're exposed to. When you add in a child's love, trust, and innocent nature, it's apparent that a parent's words can mean everything to them. Even casual barbs nonchalantly spoken from one generation to another can bring waves of trauma that take on a life of their own. My dad who is a good man, was just repeating what he inherited from his father and so on.

My dad was from India and my mom was from Pakistan. Their heritage was a constant reminder that we were different. Now deep down inside, I was proud of our diversity and empathized with my parents, whom were both refugees in a new country, but because I grew up in the United States, especially at that time, I was labeled "different." This brought with it many challenges of learning new ways which conflicted with our family's norms and traditions, as well as other assimilating obstacles. There are stereotypes of all sorts that burdened my young mind. Coupled with the fact that I was facing judgements within our family circle, as well as outside of it, I experienced a lot of confusion and insecurity.

I always felt like I was on the outside looking in from an early age. When one doesn't grasp the concept of uniqueness being a positive characteristic, it can weigh heavily on their self-worth. My parents worked long hours to put food on the table, and we, like many immigrant families, were in survival mode. The thought of aspiring higher in a professional capacity seemed far-fetched. I wasn't expected or encouraged to think bigger. In fact, like most females within the family, I was expected to be a housewife and faithfully serve my future husband. This thought process didn't bode well with me, something inside told me there was more than this. I saw girls and women who were strong and outspoken in America and knew there was something more, something better.

It was a confusing time because I always felt like the "odd girl out." It was obvious that I looked different than my classmates. The girls in my school, on television, and in magazines certainly didn't look like me, and that fact stared me in the face daily. Words like "cultured" or "exotic" weren't in vogue terms at that time, and there were constant reminders that I didn't fit in. In a neighborhood where there wasn't a lot of cultural diversity, our family also stood out by how we looked, how we spoke, what we ate, etc. Although these cultural differences should be celebrated and revered, they weren't always viewed that way. We have come a long way (and yet still have far to go) with regard to acceptance, but I certainly felt like I didn't fit in and it weighed heavily on me.

"This is the way it has always been" is a dangerous phrase, especially to a young and impressionable mind. It places limits and boxes one in without any explanation as to why "it is and always has been." Instead, a phrase that inspires and educates so that cultural and generational limitations can be broken--would do wonders to a child's perspective. If you tell a child that "they can't" enough times, one of two things could happen: they might just believe you, stunting their mindset right then and there. Or they'll figure it out, either through attrition or defiance, and find a way to prove you wrong! It takes someone who thinks differently and acts upon it in order to make change.

A few memories from my youth impacted my mindset. They weren't the most positive experiences, but when we are making a paradigm shift, we learn from both the good and bad. I vividly recall a family get-together where all the females, including myself, spent most of the day preparing a large meal. There was a lot of time and energy spent making everything look and taste just right. Dinner was served, and it was time to enjoy the fruits of our labor. Anxious to dive in, I was shocked when I was reminded that the females must serve the men first and wait until they were fully satisfied and finished before we could eat. I was furious inside, not to mention super hungry, and I just knew this was wrong! That day, I vowed this would never be acceptable in my adult life. It was like a light came on, an awakening of sorts that empowered me to carve my own path as well as create my own rules.

I knew my inability to accept my family's cultural rules was partly because I had been exposed to two vastly different worlds. But at the same time, I also felt a fire burning inside that slowly gave me confidence. I was getting a life education from what I read, saw, and experienced, and it forced me to begin creating my own set of possibilities. For example, I loved basketball as a young girl and would play at the local court. I developed a pretty good skill set and found it was a great outlet for me physically and mentally. However, it was frowned upon in our culture for girls to play a "boy's" sport as it was not ladylike, but I didn't care. I loved basketball and played it every free moment I had.

Later in high school, I tried out for the team and made it! I was elated-- it was the first time where I felt like I fit in and was part of something I could be proud of. I was small in stature but I was quick and aggressive and I deserved a spot on the starting squad. However, I learned very quickly that the players who had parents that were involved and offered their time and money to support the program received preferential treatment. Demoted to second string, I sat on the bench and watched teammates with inferior abilities start each games. It didn't seem fair, but I knew there was nothing I could do about it except to try to stay positive and do my best during practices. Unfortunately, I wasn't the only one affected by these questionable decisions and motives. They could have impacted the success of the team as a whole, too. I'll never know what could have been because my parents didn't have the time to be involved or go to my games as they were constantly working to keep us afloat. On top of that, we didn't have the financial means to give back to the school.

These were a few life lessons that helped shape my resilience as I was learning that words like "no" or "can't" or "impossible" weren't the final say. I was told I wasn't good enough to make the starting lineup but I knew I was. I was told I wasn't pretty enough, but I saw beauty inside myself and when I looked in the mirror. I was told I wasn't smart enough, but I studied and worked hard and I gained knowledge, while peeling back layer upon layer of antiquated thinking and generational and cultural trauma.

As a young child I watched, listened and believed a lot of what I heard because it was being told to me by mostly adults, within circles, and even my own peers. There were direct hits aimed at me by people I looked up to and even respected, so it was difficult to navigate through what was real in my early years. It becomes real in the mind of a young person once they accept it as true. Children believe what they hear, and if told many times over, it can become engrained in their psyche. It is a form of abuse and because it is such a vicious cycle between generations the culprits who are spewing this often don't even realize the damage they are perpetuating among the young minds around them. Whispers in circles, family get-togethers that accentuate "the way of the world" and victim mentality thinking are impactful to those within earshot of this negativity.

Maybe it was because I heard those toxic things so many times that they somehow began to lose their value. Yes, the words stung as constant reminders of feeling odd and even below average at times. However, I began figuring out that there was a great big world out there, and I would also witness glimmers of hope through contrasting experiences at home, in school, even on the playground that filtered in while offering me some positive reinforcement, even if it was just me thinking and talking to myself. I didn't realize it initially, but a certain resilience was kicking in. Possibly an innate sense of rebellion too had me questioning the very words that used to hit me like a ton of bricks.

I began trying harder at the smallest things like dribbling the basketball, my homework, my inner thoughts, and even though it was coming from an "I'll show them" type of mentality, this newfound attitude and energy offered some momentum. If I fell down, I'd dust myself off and try again because after all, there wasn't a lot expected of me through the eyes of others so I felt I had nothing to lose, and in a strange way this empowered me as I flew under the radar and began pushing through some of the muck that surrounded me. Yes, admittedly I wanted to prove to those around me that they were wrong about me.

I did feel different and looked different but that wasn't going to weaken me, rather, it strengthens me. My young mind may not have fully realized what was happening at the time, but I believed the results of my actions and not the words that were being thrown at me.

In the quiet moment of reflection, I often thought of the girl I once was—the meek, awkward soul who carried the invisible weight of generations before her. The echoes of cultural expectations, the unspoken rules of how a woman should behave, the fear of scarcity and the shadow of financial worry—all had once defined my world. But through every stumble, heartbreak, and defiant act of courage, I learned that my worth was not inherited through suffering but forged in the fire of my own becoming. The traditions that once held me back became lessons I could honor without being bound by them. And as the years unfolded, I began to see myself not as a survivor of those chains, but as the one who broke them—rising, scarred yet strong, into a life of my own making.

That awakening marked the turning point. The following years became a quiet rebellion of purpose—I poured my restless energy into school, channeling the "odd girl out" feeling that once isolated me into a fierce determination to rise above expectation. While others dismissed my dreams or whispered their judgements, I learned to let their voices sharpen my resolve rather than wound my spirit. By the time graduation loomed, the same girl who once shrank into the background had decided she would chart her own path forward. And in an unexpected twist of courage I chose the military—not as an escape, but as a declaration: I would meet the world head-on, on my own terms.

Through my journey, I began to understand that even though I wouldn't always be accepted as part of a circle, I could use my work ethic, knowledge, and resilience to break out of the mold that others had placed upon me. I stopped wondering why things were the way they were and began facing each challenge with a new, more exciting phrase: "Why not?!" This newfound mantra helped me forge ahead and go for my dreams. There would be many challenges along the way, but I was equipping myself with the tools necessary to overcome each obstacle. Slowly, but surely, I was breaking out of the self-imposed chains that held me back, while also busting out of the familial and traditional chains that had always been told were unbreakable.

In the process, it was me who became unbreakable!

CHAPTER 2

"Link by Link"

Every mosaic has pieces of the proverbial puzzle that begin to make sense as they become part of the bigger picture. I believe our journey is made up of many little pieces that represent the body of work that makes up our lives. Each tile, or piece, is part of us: our experiences, our relationships, our purpose/gift, and our legacy. Since I was a young girl, I knew there was a bigger picture, and I was determined to paint that picture, even though it wasn't clear what that would be. I wasn't always sure how I was going to accomplish my goals, but I knew I would create a personal piece of art that I could truly call my own.

Some good came out of those difficult times, and it helped shape the person I was becoming. I had proven to myself that regardless of the naysayers and doubters, —I was in control of my future. Through all the crossfire and negativity of my early years, I was lucky because I eventually recognized that change is possible. Maybe somewhere before me in my ancestral lineage, a grandmother or aunt, possibly my mom, or other female family member felt the same urge to break out, but due to the deeper restraints of their time, it was impossible. I like to believe their spirit called out and pulsed through me.

I learned that I was strong enough and worthy enough to be somebody of value who could contribute to this world.

"After all, I am the only me there is and others can say all they want, but they don't know who I really am or what I'm capable of!"

I got to that point where I refused to connect myself with what others say or think, and I no longer would give anybody access to that part of me that was once influenced by the opinions of people who chose to be victims. I no longer waited for anybody's approval or disapproval. I did, however, use some of the oppressive comments like: "You'll be a housewife who'll serve your husband," as motivation to never look back and fall victim to the vicious cycle. Those words, like fingernails to a chalkboard, still irritate me, but I don't give them power anymore. Instead, they are reminders that I have pulled away from the pack and have not fallen into the trap of archaic and misogynistic beliefs that have been perpetuated through generations.

While still in high school, I continued focusing on my studies and gained the knowledge and results that propelled my education and opened my mind to other possibilities and opportunities. I thought about the idea of pursuing a profession that would have me traveling and making a difference in some capacity. I wasn't quite sure exactly where that would lead me, but college crossed my mind as a possible next step. The medical field intrigued me, but it stayed on the back burner of my mind at the time. Through it all my grades were improving, and I was slowly building confidence and gaining momentum.

I had a few friends who were part of our quirky crew, and we laughed a lot and reminded each other that we didn't need to fit into the typical mold. Both in school and on the basketball courts,

I was aligning myself with friends who were like-minded. We had a healthy competition on the court and an air of good conversation off the court. It was a small circle, but I began to understand the importance of being part of something positive. Basketball was a great outlet for me, and I was becoming physically and mentally fit through it. Just like most teenage years, there is peer pressure and having the right people in your corner certainly helps in staving off unhealthy decisions. I smile as I recall conversations, particularly with an older boy who always seemed to be around during those years, especially at the basketball courts. His nickname was Sam, but I always referred to him by his birth name, Salem. He was more mature than the other boys and possessed a knowledge that was far beyond his years. As time went on, Salem became a good friend and a mentor of sorts whose words of encouragement were not only timely in the face of the pressures of youth, but also served as the first time anybody uttered such words as:

"You're better than this."

"You're smart and have a bright future."

"You should follow your dreams."

Never before had anybody, especially a male, seen me for me and what I was capable of. Salem's words were a reminder of my resilience and self-worth. In him, I had found a good friend and ally, as well as an overall positive figure in my life.

These small victories were proving to be big for me, because I was feeling a shift in my life as I was becoming removed from that little girl who felt insecure and unsure of herself. I understood that all the horrible things negative people had once said about me had more to do with their evolution, or lack thereof, and nothing to do with me. They were speaking from their fears and unwillingness to go after what they wanted. I knew I wouldn't make that mistake!

I continued to become a seeker of knowledge through school and life experiences. Not wanting anything to disrupt my future, I refrained from the teenage trap of partying and carelessness. While I had something to prove to myself, I'd be lying if I said that I didn't have a bit of a chip on my shoulder from those who doubted me. Maybe it was a bit petty, but I wanted to show them how wrong they really were. Using their words as fuel, I was able to channel their negative comments into a positive catalyst for the pursuit of a better life. Anytime I faced a challenge or a moment of trepidation, I would simply recall the echoes of their words, and it redirected me back to mission mode.

My decision to join the military was me using my voice in a way that would forever impact my path. As a high school senior casually strolling to the kiosk where a recruiter from the military visited our campus, I didn't know at that time I would make such a bold decision to pursue the Air Force after graduation. However, the embers had been slowly burning inside me to do something that would empower me and place me in a situation where I would have to face my fears, but also serve my country, all while guaranteeing I would expand my horizons. There would be no turning back once I signed on the dotted line and that's exactly what I needed. There are opportunities along our journey, and if we're not prepared for them, they simply drift away into what "could've" or "should've" been moments in our lives. This was one of them. I didn't realize it at the time but through the blood, sweat, and tears of my formative years, I was galvanizing myself to make such bold decisions. Certainly, this would be considered a rebellious move on my part, but I had built up a strong defense against what others may think.

Maybe I was rebelling against all the stuff I saw and heard over the years as others constantly told me what I should or shouldn't do and, what was expected of me. The Air Force had high expectations and offered a challenge while evoking a symbol of strength, which truly appealed to me.

At first, I made the decision because it was a way out of the boxed-in environment that surrounded me. There was a great big world out there with places to see, people to meet, and experiences to be had and I possessed a burning desire to be a part of that. I was also deeply proud to serve in the military, for I knew it was a big part of the very freedom that allowed me to choose a better life. I'm not quite sure I understood the scope of danger and fear I'd be facing, but I'd soon find out. Needless to say, my family was shocked and not particularly excited about my decision. Once again, their lack of understanding and support filled the air. However, the once powerful words that had inflicted doubt, fear, and insecurity years before now fell upon deaf ears.

Over time, I learned to separate the truth from the noise. The cutting words, the sideways glances, the disbelief that once pierced me so deeply—all of it began to sound different when I understood where it came from. Deep down inside, their doubts were never truly about me, but about what my growth revealed in them. Family and so-called friends who had once comforted themselves by keeping me small began to see me rise as an uncomfortable mirror. It took strength to forgive them, and even greater strength to move beyond the need for their approval. In that understanding, I found freedom more profound than any external validation—an unshakable clarity that my path was mine alone to walk, no longer hindered by their limited vision.

That clarity would become my armor in years ahead. When the desert heat of Iraq pressed down like a living thing, when exhaustion and fear whispered in my ear, I called upon that same courage that once carried me through the quiet wars of my youth. The Air Force tested me in ways I could never have imagined, but it also refined my sense of purpose. Each mission, each dawn that broke over foreign soil, reminded me that strength wasn't the absence of fear, it was the decision to move forward anyway. And just as I had done all my life, I pressed on, steadfast, evolving, and alive with fierce knowledge that I was no longer the girl who needed to prove myself, but the woman who already had.

Step by step, piece by piece, the mosaic of my life was taking shape, and the making of something beautiful was in the works. For the first time in my life, I was truly proud of what I saw; I liked who I was and where I was going. Things were fitting into place, and the picture I was painting brought joy to my soul. Salem was right, I did have a bright future, and this newfound sense of control, empowered me. Although I was still a work in progress, like we all are, I was becoming a breaker of the chain; those generational shackles that held back so many before me were being destroyed. That vicious cycle would not include me as a statistical casualty. All of these experiences were part of my new mindset, and they emboldened me while reiterating the fact that there is a better way!

CHAPTER 3

"The War Zone"

Those early experiences had a profound effect on me, yet somehow, I survived. Maybe it was ignorance, spite, or just a resilience I didn't know I had, but I'm grateful I emerged stronger. If I had the choice to change the manner in which I gained this experience from all that I endured, I absolutely would. But I can't go back and make others do things differently. All I can do is make sure I do things differently and expose the causes of such vicious cycles and teach others the steps to overcome trauma. Through it all, thankfully, I was still standing, and at 18 years old, I was able to distinguish between right and wrong with the clarity of an older, wiser person. I was in a pretty good place to face the next chapter of my life, which would be in the United States Air Force.

I'm not sure how prepared any teenager can be for the mental and physical demands of the military, and I was certainly no exception. However, I had been battle-tested from my early years, and a stronger version of myself had resurrected. Ironically, the very experiences which broke me down time after time as a child, now served me well with regard to toughness. I had an outlook of "nothing to lose," and the fear of failing and falling down was no longer front and center in my mind.

Being an underdog was certainly nothing new to me, as I had become accustomed to that role. In fact, there was (and still is) a part of me that thrives in this environment. There is a "Tell me I can't, and watch me prove you wrong" sort of mindset that is evoked in me when challenged. I was not only the first person in my family to serve, but I was also a South Asian female entering a predominantly male world. I had something to prove (again), at least in my own mind, and I vowed to put my best foot forward. Better yet, I would use my best foot to kick down any barrier that got in my way! I was far removed from that beaten-down, subservient, insecure girl I had once been. In some ways, I was well-equipped for the task ahead, as I had lived as an underdog for the last 18 years. It was no surprise that I would find myself as an underdog once again.

However, what was surprising to me, and to a certain degree, refreshing, was that I wasn't alone in this regard; the military in large part is made up of people from all walks of life and experiences, including gender, race, and religion. In some ways, the very people that were considered outcasts in civilian society are the brave soldiers risking their lives for the maintenance of freedom for a society that had previously cast them out. It's an irony which has long intrigued me. I was no longer the odd girl out, as we were a community of outcasts and oddballs facing our fears, while growing up together.

Boot camp without question challenged me, and by no means did I breeze through it, but the mettle I developed from those difficult times in my youth seemed to serve me well in the way of mental and physical preparation. I recall facing those traditional exercises meant to break down young cadets for the purposes of later rebuilding, and I wasn't caught off guard like some of the others were. I didn't take it personally when "spat" upon and yelled at with verbal assaults. I had basically seen it all in my previous world, so this was nothing new. I now possessed the capacity to distinguish different intents. In fact, there was a part of me that thrived in this environment because it challenged me to prove myself once again. I smile as I recall an officer's attempt to test me with push-ups, sit-ups, and other physical exercises thinking I may be weak—only to show him I was up for the challenge. The look on his face of shock, which later turned to defeat, as he gestured to me to carry on, was very fulfilling as I knocked out each task without breaking much of a sweat. I wouldn't be broken; I couldn't be broken because I had already been broken down to pieces and rebuilt stronger from what I endured early on.

That moment stayed with me long after the dust of boot camp settled. It wasn't about proving to anyone else, it was about proving to myself that I belonged, that my strength was no accidental circumstance but a choice I made every day. So, when it was time to fulfill my call of duty, I didn't shrink from the uncertainties ahead. The lessons of discipline, resilience, and quiet confidence would now follow me beyond the training fields, across oceans and into the unforgiving deserts of Iraq. What awaited me there would test my courage in ways no drill ever could, but I was ready. Every push-up, every challenge, every moment of doubt conquered had led me there—to the next chapter of my becoming.

I found a sense of community within the Air Force, as well as a sense of pride. I grew into a different person while serving and faced different fears than before, but I was part of something bigger than myself for the first time in my life, and I wasn't alone. I felt a sense of pride and honor, which I was reminded of for the first time as I strolled along the River Walk in San Antonio while on break. I was in uniform, and person after person thanked me for my service. I wasn't prepared for this outpouring of gratitude directed at me, as it was a complete opposite dynamic from what I was accustomed to. The sentiments were so genuine that they touched me deep inside. I was the one grateful for the opportunity, yet others were thanking me. These were reminders that I was definitely on the right track, and there was a sense of direction and purpose in my life. I felt good, and it gave me pause for thought as I reflected on those conversations I had with myself over and over again as a child trying to pep talk myself into overcoming a difficult situation. This time, the tears were joyful ones and the words that I spoke to myself were: "I'm proud of you!"

Of course, there were some shocking moments, as well, like that first time I was told I would be deployed to Iraq. It was a complete 180-degree different conversation than that of my recruiter who said "That would never happen." But happened it did, and although I was scared, I knew this was part of my journey and I would face my fears head on. There was even a sense of excitement for what was ahead, backed by the principle of a good cause. Deployment gave me time to think—long nights beneath foreign skies, where the hum of distant generators and the scent of sand reminded me how far I'd come. Amid the chaos, I began to see my life with a new kind of clarity. The military had taught me discipline, but I realized that true freedom would come from knowledge. Education, I now understood, was the master key—the way to break the cycles that had bound my family and so many others to struggle. If I could master my mind the way I mastered my will, I could not only rewrite my own story but light a path for others to follow.

While in Iraq, we soldiers bonded through our common purpose and even tumult. We experienced our war zones within a war zone; it was there that I first recognized the pressures placed on the human mind and how we are affected by what we're exposed to. I knew this all too well in my own life, but seeing others dealing with anxiety, fear, homesickness and depression was altogether a different animal. We talked through a lot of this together and shared our feelings, which helped. We were in this fight together, but I wondered what would happen to some of us should we be fortunate enough to survive this war zone and return to civilian life back home. How would some of us assimilate? I had a strong feeling that some of my fellow soldiers would need therapy post-military.

I saw a lot during this experience, including a memorable moment when a bomb went off super close to where we were stationed, and the impact shook me both physically and emotionally. In fact, it was a rocket bomb that blew up within yards of where we were, while decimating four large gas tanks and a building, as well as creating an explosion that could be heard for miles. It was something I'll never forget, and the thought of life and death crossed my mind in a way that changed me. This was real, and I thought to myself "I can't die here. I can't die yet." I thank God to this day that my story didn't end there. I remember thinking "things were beginning to go my way, and I have so much to live for!" It also reminded me how so many good people I met in the military were not only risking their lives each moment, but they were also affected by what they experienced. The feelings of relief that came when the danger subsided opened my eyes and mind to be "on purpose" with my life. A new sense of urgency set in, and shortly thereafter I decided that

I would be a part of a movement in my own life and the lives of others' as well. I would utilize the opportunities the military afforded me in the way of education, and go to college when I returned. My journey into the medical profession was born while I was in the Air Force, and this decision excited me, and also brought with it a different set of fears and challenges.

I was going to become a doctor someday, and although I recall the medical profession crossing my mind back in high school, as I was intrigued with anatomy class and discussions from would-be doctors who spoke at our school, I knew that I would have to work harder than ever to accomplish this goal. I couldn't cruise through school like I did back home, kind of getting by fairly easily without showing much interest or effort. Medical school would become another type of war zone in my life, but this time my drive was backed by a definitiveness of purpose that I hadn't known before. I used to be driven by survival, which helped me escape an unruly environment, but I now had a passion with a higher purpose: I wanted to help others! I began to understand the scope of difficulty so many people are facing with their mental health, as well as the triggers. I was confident this was my calling and that "I'll show them" mentality ignited me once again, but this time it was deeper.

I couldn't help but remember a conversation I had with my then, so-called best friend, Sarah, back in high school when I shared with her the idea of my attending college. She casually reminded me that "You have to be smart to go to college!" Another "stupid" slur that once hurt me, but now propelled me to prove anybody who ever doubted me (including myself), wrong! Needless to say, the "Sarah's" of the world are no longer in my life...by choice! In many ways my exposure to negative words, people, and lifestyles helped me to become an optimist. I recognized the power of positivity and was proving to myself that if I put my mind to something, especially if I believed in it—then there wasn't anybody or anything that could get in the way of accomplishing my goals. While others were focusing on the negative, and counter-productive activity, I focused on possibilities and solutions.

In some ways I experienced a sort of war zone of my own during those early years. Through all the negativity, doubt, and pain—I had survived! I'm reminded how delicate and nuanced our childhood can be, and the influence and habits that are developed. Our exposure to trauma can rear its ugly head in many different ways, especially if steps are not taken to remedy them. I'm not sure if I'd call it luck, but I certainly feel lucky that I have taken a different route and created a life that I'm proud of. By no means is it an easy fix, especially when the odds are stacked against you through the words and actions of others. However, like many remedies, it begins with knowledge; the knowledge that, first, we're not alone, and there is help out there if you seek it. I'm still empathetic to that little girl in me who felt those feelings of not being good enough. I am compassionate to others who are experiencing their own war zone within their lives as we battle such things as anxiety, depression, and mental health challenges at an alarming rate. And I'm committed to helping others overcome, while living the very best life possible!

CHAPTER 4

"I'm Possible"

How do we enact change within ourselves so that we may live a more balanced, fulfilling, and purposeful life? There is no magic potion or quick fix, and although this fact in itself is a reminder that there is work ahead and it may not be easy, we can take solace in the knowledge that it certainly is not only possible, but it is within our own grasp. Like I mentioned before, knowledge is power! Not to over simplify such a complex subject as change, we do possess the capabilities to ensure that the very change we are seeking does not have to become an overcomplicated process. In other words, we can create the life we want, and also live the life in which we were intended, simply by our own doing, and in some cases, by our own undoing. I had a choice to perpetuate the traumas of my past into a whirlwind of struggle and victimization, or undo that which once burdened me. I chose the latter, and just like the line in Robert Frost's epic poem, "It has made all the difference."

Is it possible to overcome the emotional, physical, and generational traumas of our childhood and/or the current things we are struggling with today? I'm writing this book mainly because I have become an empowered woman/person, even though my road to getting here was strewn with one disadvantage after another. So, the answer to that question is simply, **yes!** This is not to say it has been easy, nor is it meant to pat myself on the back (okay, maybe just a little, lol), but seriously, my purpose for these words is meant to empower you. Say the word "empowerment" over and over, and you'll extract a feeling of hope. Empowerment is a word we hear more in this past decade than possibly ever before, and I believe this is a good thing. It makes me feel good saying it and writing it, and now living through its concept, because it's a strong word with a strong message. One of the definitions given within the dictionary for empowerment is: "the process of becoming stronger and more confident, especially in controlling one's life and claiming one's rights." To me, that just about says it all with regard to enacting that very change we seek. We can claim/reclaim our life!

Hope becomes faith when we are empowered and we can create a different cycle, a "victorious cycle," instead of a "vicious cycle." You chose to pick up this book and read this far because on some level besides possible curiosity, you are seeking change. You have now entered the beautiful world of empowerment because no matter what your current situation is, it can become even better as you've taken a step forward. We can all improve within our lives, whether we are enduring heavy duty challenges right now or wanting to enhance our already pretty good situation. Maybe you'll use this as a refresher course, or even share this information with others who may need some positivity and hope even more than you do. Either way, I'm grateful.

And this is how that once little, beaten-down, outsider girl became empowered—through knowledge first. Learning, even at times through many trials and errors, ultimately helped me seek a better way. I read, I learned, I applied it to my life and I not only survived, I thrived because the information I was learning, seeing, and experiencing, woke me up to the possibilities. Even though I had it tough in many ways and had to work harder than some in order to get similar results, I knew that others had it tougher, yet they succeeded. Voila! Hope then transformed into faith, and the knowledge became my own knowing that I would empower myself through and through in order to succeed and place myself in a position to make a difference within my own life, and the lives of others.

I now knew there was a goal in sight, and this drove me to take a different path and keep on moving forward. Given what I had dealt with in my past, I knew that I had to stay focused on the tasks at hand in order to reach my goals. I identified what I wanted, which was becoming a doctor so I could help others, and myself through a proud, purposeful, and stable career. My goal now became my mission, and even though there were moments in which I questioned myself and my decisions along the way, my mind had been made up, and that was what kept me going even through the toughest times. "My mind," these very words are a reminder of how powerful our brains are, because even though we hear and say "my mind," we can embrace the very essence of empowerment within our own minds. "My mind is made up." Who makes it up? We do! I made a decision to become a doctor because I could decide for myself within my own mind what I wanted to do with my life. We have choices and those choices become decisions, which if followed by action, and coupled with momentum, empower us because we are in control of ourselves. We are powerful and in charge of our lives!

As a woman, and particularly a South Asian woman who had many cultural, traditional, and financial challenges along the way, I'm even more passionate about empowering other women to create a mindset of strength and purpose. I recall several moments in my life where the idea of empowerment was an unknown concept. Even after my time in the military when I had gained some confidence and direction, I still dealt with that feeling of being viewed as an outcast. During college and even within medical school, people purposely tried making me feel awkward, and I want to make sure that I use my platform to help others embrace who they are, while becoming the best they can be.

The decision to make change and go after your goals in life isn't just a one-time thing. It can be a continuous series of events and actions that are ongoing. It took me a long time to realize that I not only had no need to "fit in," but that I didn't want to fit in to a mold others thought was cool or better. I heard the whispers and saw the looks as I delved deep into my studies so I could stay on purpose, while others were drinking and partying. I knew that eventually the invites would slow down because it became evident that I was shifting inside and found a quality group of friends with whom we shared interests and focus. It wasn't quantity that appealed to me regarding my circle, it was quality. In fact, those earlier emotions of being that odd girl out began to shift as well. There wasn't pain attached to being different, it was more of a recognition that I had bigger things to accomplish, and with that came an empowerment and ownership. I was able to realize there was a bigger picture than that. In a strange way, the abusive reminders of my past drove me to make sure I achieved more. Feeling like an outcast early in my life, even though that pain isn't something I'd wish on anyone, the role was an already familiar one so I embraced it and stayed in my own world. Now, this is not to say I didn't enjoy some moments along the way as I was working hard, because I did have plenty of fun and positive experiences too. However, there were many times I was reminded that I wasn't exactly the life of the party, but I remained diligent.

If you look at some of the great inventors, creators, artists, philanthropists, and teachers in history, there is a commonality most of them share, and it is the choice to be different—to take a different path. Some may have innately seen things differently, while others were boxed into their own corner by society, but whatever the case may be, being different for all intents and purposes, is a good thing. It took me years to strengthen myself through these feelings, but just like I was able to work through the challenges of my early years, I overcame this too through empowering myself. I was realizing moment by moment that not only was I viewed as being different, but I embraced my differences and eventually celebrated them. We humans have a lot more in common than we sometimes like to admit, like the need for love, connection, safety, esteem, expression, empathy, etc., but the small stuff like "being cool" or "popular" within cliques or on social media should not be a priority.

I took stock of who I was becoming and where I was headed. The years had stripped away the need to blend in or chase anyone else's approval. Where once I might have envied those who followed the crowd, now I looked at things differently and realized there was strength in not fitting in because it led to a path that would make a difference. It may have seemed a lonelier pursuit for someone my age, but it was one carved with intention and truth. Each challenge I faced revealed another layer of strength, and that strength became my shield against distraction. The noise of the world, the comparisons, the gossip, the fleeting temptations—no longer had power over me. For the first time, I wasn't just surviving life; I was living deliberately.

There is a higher purpose for each of us. I've often asked myself the question "Why are we here?" Although it took many years to for me to answer this, I've come to believe that not only do we have individual gifts we should seek within ourselves, but once discovered, we should share our gifts for the common good of others. More than ever, our world needs kindness and support. Let's build each other up instead of breaking each other down. Let's strengthen and not weaken. We can empower ourselves and spread the word. I sometimes look back at my life as I was, and still am, climbing that proverbial mountain, and I envision the releasing of those chains which once bound and hindered me, then finally standing tall at the top with arms stretched to the skies, I shout out for the world to hear: "I'm possible!"

That sense of purpose would guide me into the next chapter of my journey, where my focus turned fully toward education, the greater equalizer. It wasn't just about earning a degree; it was about rewriting the narrative that once limited me. In classrooms and late-night study sessions, I would come to see learning as liberation, knowledge as armor and wisdom as the true inheritance I would claim for myself and generations to follow. My mission was clear now: to transform my life through the power of education, proving that the girl who once doubted her worth had become the woman destined to change her world.

CHAPTER 5

"Education: The Equalizer"

The one thing that became abundantly clear to me through all my trials and tribulations, whether it be emotional, generational, cultural, or societal traumas, was the lifeline that education offered me as a way to rise above it all. While writing this book, I often reflected upon my past and realized that every challenge I faced was mitigated by the knowledge and strength I obtained through educating myself to understand that other people's evolution did not have to determine mine. The common denominator in providing tools needed to navigate through the painful moments in my life was found through a knowing that I could write my own life story, regardless of the cards I was dealt with. Although it took me a while to understand the concept of my own autonomy being in my grasp, I eventually propelled myself through the knowledge I found within books, mentors, life experiences, and faith.

There is a vast array of learning material available to us, now more than ever, whereby we can educate ourselves in ways never before imagined. If possible, higher education through college is certainly a great option for empowering our minds, especially through our crucial development years. Books are filled with knowledge that others have spent years researching, learning, and experiencing, and we have immediate access to their words of wisdom, through which we can learn so much. I realized through educating myself that, it didn't matter where I came from, what mattered most was where I was going. What I chose to think, act, who I associated myself with, were all choices I could make for myself. The road that was paved for me through others didn't necessarily have to become my permanent path. We are exposed to familial conditioning that sometimes can be archaic in the way of thinking, as well as damaging to our self-worth, whether the intentions are good, bad, indifferent, or just habitual. Although much good can come from what we learn from our parents, there also can exist dysfunction that affects us as a whole person. We are programmed to believe everything an adult does and says, and through a process of distinguishing/knowledge, only then can we discover what to do, and what not to do.

Each person internalizes things differently depending on their own makeup, and there is always room for improvement. Educating ourselves opens our minds to the possibilities, and can help us to denounce the previous conditioning that we were exposed to. The great minds of the past can often become some of our greatest assets when it comes to gaining knowledge in the way of their writings/research. The public library is chock full of free material that can enrich our minds with the necessary information for growth. We have to be mindful with what we digest in our psyche, while reminding ourselves that our "brain food" is just as (if not more) important than what we ingest in the way of food for our nourishment. You've probably heard the phrase, "Our body is our temple." Well, so too, is our mind!

My years in college were definitely a great learning curve, both in the way of studies as I pursued my degree in nutrition, but they also opened up a whole new world of possibilities with what I learned from a psychological and sociological standpoint. I was fortunate enough to have classes and professors that helped to shape my thinking, while also expanding my horizons as I was slowly, but surely, becoming a free-thinker. I was finding myself and discovering my purpose, as I soaked up every bit of information I could.

Although my college experience was a world away from the social mores of the high school culture, which confused me with its cliquey vibe, I still remember a few instances where those horrible feelings of being judged and stereotyped resurfaced. One scenario in particular came when I was hard at work in a class and I answered several questions correctly from our professor. Later in the class, he began chatting with me in a positive and supportive manner, while validating my knowledge. I noticed the whispers around me as a small group of students giggled and shared a meme that illustrated a "brown-nosing" student talking with the teacher, as if to say I was "kissing up" and being a teacher's pet. I tried to ignore it, but it conjured up so many rough memories from high school. This type of behavior almost broke me in my younger days, but I knew the game now and chose to laugh it off, reminding myself that I was on the right path through focus and hard work, while some others were still stuck within that box of immaturity.

We are all works in progress, and there will be moments of moving past challenges through giant leaps, baby steps, and even learning through our backward and side steps. We must keep on moving forward, both with educating our minds, while taking action toward our goals. We can develop our own resiliency while picking and choosing what nourishes and nurtures our soul. Conversely, we need to be aware of what might negatively affect our progress. There will be people and situations along the way that require our conscious decisions to accept or deny their influence. A great tool that can help you navigate through such possible scenarios is to actually visualize how you will respond to a situation in advance. Practice your responses prior to a situation unfolding like a dress rehearsal so that it isn't a foreign circumstance if and when it actually does happen, and you'll know how to handle it.

An example of information and communication that we must understand and decipher carefully, is social media. This form of sharing can be a great asset in many ways, including advertisement, social networking, and building a platform for millions to see. However, it can also be very toxic in the way of normalizing an unhealthy and unrealistic lifestyle. Cyber bullying, targeting, conditioning through exposure of a reality TV-type dynamic can open up Pandora's Box with a plethora of negative emotional influences. We must equip ourselves with the right armor of recognition to fend off possible modes of triggers, and we can do this through an open mind of learning.

Some people have used this form of media with honorable intentions, while spreading positivity. Unfortunately, there are some that are a big part of the problem, rather than solution, when it comes to breaking others down, instead of helping to build them up. Social media has become such a gravitational pull for so many of our youth that parents are dealing with an entirely different set of challenges when teaching their children right from wrong. Kids (and adults) are seeking approval in the way of likes and followers, while placing too much importance on what others think, all within a "meta verse" world. Set your standards high when it comes to what or whom you allow access with regard to your whole self, while not allowing frivolous distractions on your journey for balance.

In addition to our basic human needs, we also have emotional needs that are part and parcel of our balance and well-being. Being loved, feeling accepted and secure are certainly vital components that feed our mind, body, and spirit. Who and what we allow, in the way of access to ourselves, is a discernment that should not be taken lightly. In other words, we are the captain of our own ship; the crew we allow on board, who gives us the best chance of a prosperous journey, as we navigate the "sea of life" is entirely up to us! I have found myself in the "wrong room" a few times when it comes to choosing circles or centers of influence. Now, I just walk out of those "rooms," when I realize the group/clique will not be good for my soul. I pick and choose my "rooms" carefully these days.

College became more than a return to the classroom; it was proving ground for my mind and spirit. The long nights spent studying, the quiet mornings filled with reflection, and the constant balancing act between academic demands and life's responsibilities all shaped me in ways no textbook could. I began to see how discipline and purpose, when married with curiosity, could ignite something unstoppable. Each paper turned in, every exam conquered, was another testament to the power of follow-through, the same grit that once carried me through boot camp and the battlefield now fueled my pursuit of knowledge. The "school of life," as I came to call it, taught me that inspiration isn't a fleeting spark; it's a steady flame, fed by perspective and belief in one's purpose.

I was blessed to have earned a degree from the University of Texas at Austin, with a B.S. in Nutrition, and I was certainly proud of this accomplishment. I continued my educational journey and achieved my M.S. in Medical Science at the University North Texas Health Science Center. Years of focus, sacrifice, and relentless drive, despite my early obstacles led to the moment when I received an acceptance letter to medical school. Holding it in my hands I felt a surge of emotions—a mix of gratitude, disbelief, and quiet pride. This was no accident or stroke of luck. It was the result of every lesson, every sleepless night, every promise I made to myself to rise. That little girl that was knocked down, time after time, from the words and judgements of others, was on her way to medical school! The University of Pikeville, Kentucky College of Osteopathic Medicine would be by next stop.

It didn't stop there, as I worked tirelessly in my pursuit of becoming a doctor in internal medicine. That flame would only burn brighter as I set my sights higher. The idea of becoming a doctor, once distant and almost impossible, had now become my compass. As I prepared to step into the next chapter, I knew this was more than a career choice, it was my calling made real! The inscription of each milestone along my journey of empowerment all had one common theme etched upon them: knowledge! Whether it be a formal education through college or trade school, and/or self-education through a desire for knowledge, it is incumbent upon each and every one of us to rise above any obstacle that life throws at us by embracing the great equalizer: education!

CHAPTER 6

"Pillars"

Continuing my educational path, I entered medical school with a renewed sense of purpose and empowerment. It dawned on me that I had actually overcome seemingly impossible odds and was that much closer to reaching my goal of becoming a doctor. Through trial and error, the life knowledge I obtained up to that point propelled me forward. Not because I was blessed with inherent gifts that made my path easy, but quite the opposite—the very things that I did not allow to defeat me actually made me stronger. This clarity through resilience was a powerful reminder that we are stronger and more capable than we may think. Believe me, it wasn't easy, through the "sticks and stones" hurled my way from an early age, as roadblocks were strewn about my path at seemingly every turn. There will always be obstacles along our journey, and some may have it rougher than others in different forms, perhaps through the disadvantaged cards that are dealt from an early age. However, when there's a will, there's a way, and if we understand this life mantra with an open mind, education/empowerment, as well as a willingness to remain diligent and focused, we certainly can embolden ourselves to create our own path along the way.

As I sat down to write this book, I did a lot of reflection about not only the tough times, but also some key principles that helped me overcome all those challenges. Every building or structure must have within it a strong foundation that keeps it standing, even in stormy climates. It is the same for us as people; we must have mettle that is fortified inside us, weathered properly, that can stand the test of time. This strength/resilience is crucial to keeping us from breaking down into rubble. Also, there must be a certain give, because life will push us, pull us, and try to expose our weaknesses. Balance comes into play as a natural neutralizer to the elements around us. Yes, concrete, metal, iron, etc., are important parts of the foundation, but bamboo is strong too, and it can serve well as a bending aspect that helps us to adjust to those moments in our lives that require strength, but also flexibility.

We can nurture our bodies and minds from an inside-out perspective, much like a tree built from the ground up. We all might take a simple tree for granted because they are all around us and always have been. We might have climbed them as a child, swung from a tire on their branch, or picked fruit from one in our yard. So many great things come from a tree, including necessary-to-life oxygen. Look at how strong that tree is, how tall it stands, how old it may be, and what it has been exposed to. Where does its resilience and strength come from? There may be hundreds, if not thousands, of little and big roots underneath that provide its foundation. These roots serve as pillars of strength underneath it all, while the beauty and above-ground structure of the tree is all we may notice, the heart and soul of the tree can be found within its roots. Think of these principles as your roots, your pillars of strength that will enhance your life with structure, balance, and flexibility:

OPEN YOUR MIND

Without an open mind, any possibility of change or progress will fall upon deaf ears. Very few things in this life are certainties; most of the information we receive on a daily basis can be classified as conjecture, opinions, and, at times, even bred from ulterior motives. It shouldn't be an "us versus them" mindset, when actually the biggest distractors ultimately lie in an "us versus us" dilemma as we get in our own way, especially in the era of social media and the political climate in which we find ourselves. This can not only be distracting, but also damaging to our whole self. The "Reality TV" mindset is all around us, and it is toxic as some people believe the drama and dysfunction is okay. Set your own standards, and you'll come to realize very soon that all those little things that bogged you down with worry were inconsequential and petty.

BREATHE

Take that deep breath and inhale through your nose, now hold it for a few seconds, then exhale slowly through your pursed lips. Repeat 5 to 10 times and do this a few times a day. Do you notice your body slowly relaxing itself? It takes about 30 seconds to regulate your nervous system and a simple tool with the breath, which is with you all the time, can be your best friend. This may seem like a small exercise in the whole scheme of things with what you are facing in the way of fear, anxiety, and uncertainty, but it is a great way to slow things down and put them in perspective through a physiological and psychological manner. We require breath for life, and we can purposefully change the way we breathe—thus, change the way we breathe in all that we are exposed to, while becoming the best version of ourselves on our journey of life. Taking that moment to inhale during any situation before reaction or overreaction can also be a game changer with regard to the best possible outcome. Five seconds to breathe and assess before losing your temper and/or acting out makes for a peaceful life.

NOURISHMENT

Nourishing ourselves through food and water is not just about survival, it's about communication. Every bite, every sip, every thought sends biochemical messages that either heal or harm. In functional medicine, nourishment is the foundation of optimal health. The foods we consume directly influence our **gut microbiome,** the trillions of microbes that live within us and dictate everything from digestion and detoxification to mood, hormones, and immunity. When we eat real, whole, unprocessed foods, we feed a diverse, balanced microbiome that supports energy, clarity, and emotional resilience. When we consume processed foods, refined sugars, or artificial additives, we shift that microbial balance toward inflammation, keeping us in a cycle of fatigue, cravings, and low mood.

This is the essence of the **gut-brain-axis,** a two-way communication system between your enteric nervous system (the "second brain" in your gut) and your central nervous system. About 90% of serotonin, your body's feel-good neurotransmitter, is made in the gut. That means your mood, sleep, focus, and even motivation is all influenced by what you eat and how well your gut ecosystem functions.

But nourishment doesn't stop at the plate. What we feed our minds and spirits matters just as deeply. The energy of our environment, the conversation we have, the media we consume, and the company we keep, all shape our internal chemistry. Chronic exposure to negativity or comparison activates the same stress pathways that drive inflammation in the body. True nourishment is holistic: body, mind, and spirit. It's choosing meals that support cellular repair, thoughts that promote peace, and people who inspire expansion. It's hydrating not just with water, but with positive energy, purpose, and presence. And remember, sometimes you'll find yourself in the "wrong room." A room that drains your energy, dulls your light, or feeds fear instead of faith. You have every right to gracefully step out and walk toward the room that restores your alignment. When we nourish ourselves well—physically and energetically—we shift from survival mode to creation mode. That's where true healing begins.

SELF-CARE

This is another level of nourishing our whole self as we feed our soul. Massages, facials, meditation, yoga, hiking, etc., are no longer viewed as luxuries. These, and other methods of self-care are vital components to creating balance in our lives. Something as simple as a nice stroll through the park or even a 20-minute walk through your neighborhood does wonders for your well-being. Proper sleep is a part of self-care, too, and even though it's a necessity and probably something most of us take for granted, getting enough good sleep will greatly affect every other aspect of our life. Small changes in your physical and mental activity bring big changes in your overall quality of life. There are time constraints in each of our lives and schedule demands that will always be there. However, prioritizing that 15-minute morning stretch, 20-minute walk, 30-minute massage, 1-minute breathing exercise, can make a world of difference. Self-care can invigorate your senses and give you a more positive perspective as well.

I remember trying yoga while in college, and I noticed how helpful it was for me while dealing with the anxiety, stress, and fear that was all around me at the time. After experiencing panic attacks from taking my MCAT test, the inner peace I received from yoga was my savior, as it truly helped to mitigate the negative stuff, and before I knew it, I felt more balance and energy. Anxiety was literally affecting my life and progress at the time because I literally shutdown from panic of testing and I just couldn't get through the MCATs. The demands of schooling, especially during my time in medical school, were daunting, and I had to find ways that could not only give me the best possible chance for success with my studies and future career, but also maximize my ability to retain the information of the curriculum, while making the most of every moment of my time. Yoga, meditation, exercise, and positive mental nourishment provided the edge I needed, while feeding my soul and strengthening my body. After several attempts, I finally passed! It was yoga that not only got me through but also opened my eyes to a different path of healing; the allopathic way of resorting to prescription drugs isn't always the answer, there are alternatives that heal from within, and yoga was exactly that for me. I slept better, felt better, learned better, and I had balance, even while facing an arduous schedule that came with high emotional, physical, and psychological demands. I was learning not only how to practice medicine, but I was learning how to be a more balanced, nurturing, and soulful person. I continue to practice yoga and breathing exercises in my daily life.

These principles became my pillars—steady anchors I could return to when the world felt heavy. Open-mindedness reminds us that wisdom requires humility, that every encounter is an opportunity to learn and expand. Let breathing become your daily reset, a reminder that calm and clarity can be reclaimed in even the most chaotic moments. Nourishment, for both body and mind, teaches us that strength is sustained through care, not depletion—that the foods we eat, the thoughts we feed ourselves, and the people we surround ourselves with all shape our vitality. And self-care, once mistaken for indulgence, became my act of self-respect, the practice of replenishing my energy so I can continue serving with purpose. Self-care is often overlooked and sometimes viewed as a luxury rather than a necessity. We must retool our thinking when it comes to self-care, and we should embrace it as part of our preventative and integrative care. These pillars certainly helped prepare me for medical school; they became the quiet framework for a life built on balance, resilience and intention. Try and visualize each pillar as your foundation that will provide strength and support as you add balance to your daily life. Be aware of your presence in this life through gratitude and add these pillars as part of your foundation.

Our life is made up of millions of different moments, and if we recognize that we are the ones in the driver's seat of most of these moments, we will not only see life with more clarity, fulfillment, and purpose, but we can also appreciate these moments with more zest than ever before. We've heard the cliché' "life is short!" and though in the whole scheme of things it may be, it also can be viewed as a gift from possibly a higher source (depending on your beliefs), and we can dictate the time we have been blessed with in order to maximize our moments, while helping others to do the same. For some reason, we are here, and we are an energy source that can determine how much light we emit inside and out. I don't have the scientific answer as to why we are here, but I do know we can each make the most of our time while we are here!

CHAPTER 7

"Authenticity"

The progression of who I once was to who I was becoming seemed to shock even myself. Unlike most chapters of life that may unfold slowly over time through a sequence of several small ebbs and flows, mine came upon me like a huge crashing wave. At least my acknowledgment of my progress hit me all at once through a reflective lens. I'm sure that certain milestones or major accomplishments for some are recognized through the compliment of others. For example, if somebody has a noticeable weight loss transformation, people tend to verbalize their reaction to such change with a, "Wow, you look great! How did you do it? Good for you!" sort of response. This can be validating, as our achievements are commended. Mine hit me one day as I was sitting in the front row (by choice) of medical school listening to the professor while taking in the information. I realized I'm now in the front row by my own choosing, because I'm not only interested in learning and growing, but I'm confident enough, if called upon, to answer any questions thrown my way. This in itself shocked me because it was evidence of how far I'd come. I now possessed a noticeable sense of confidence that was rooted in knowledge not only from an academia standpoint, but also what I call "Life 101." The symbolism spoke to me as I was now front row and center of my life and future.

I was no longer bogged down by what others thought of me, as I had fully embraced who I was and who I was becoming. This was empowering in and of itself. I was less impressed by the façade of others trying to build themselves up while knocking me down, and more impressed being comfortable in my own skin. The very skin that once differentiated myself from others, and caused me insecurity, was now my formidable ally in the sense that it belonged to me and I to it, and I was proud of this distinction. Mostly, I was proud of that little girl who didn't always fit in, didn't quite seem "good enough," who was now a woman that had become "more than enough" in my own eyes, and not requiring the acceptance of others for validation. Like most journeys, it came with bumps and bruises, as well as hard-learned life lessons. However, I chose to perceive and receive those challenging times as fortifiers of my own strength.

Our education is ongoing whether it be intentional through books, academia, and/or through our life experiences. As I sat down to write this book, a few things stood out to me as profound reminders that positively impacted my growth:

- "The evolution of others does not have to become my evolution."
- "Always be authentic."
- "Take things into my own hands."

We've mentioned generational trauma and vicious cycles throughout this book because it is important to impress upon the fact that they often go unrecognized, and they often go hand in hand as mindsets, traditions, and "that's how it's always been" mentality that toxically transfers from one generation to another, thus perpetuating the cycle of digression. Again, I'm proud of my heritage and many of the cultural diversities that are inherent within it, and I recognize and respect the differences in other cultures and ethnicities, as well as understand the importance of acknowledging our ancestors in ways that impact us in positive ways. However, with some of these traditions comes archaic and oppressive ways of thinking, which I choose not to be a participant of. Some of these ways are more obvious than others, while others are more subtle. Either way, if they are damaging, hurtful, or misogynistic in nature, then it is counter to the way I choose to live my life. In fact, my path has been partly carved in spite of such thinking. We can choose to be part of the solution or part of the problem, and I choose to be an example of what a strong woman of color and ethnicity can accomplish with an empowering mindset, while leaving those old, antiquated, and regressive ideas in my dust! Remember, "Just because things are the way they are, that doesn't mean they have to continue to be that way."

Through it all there was an understanding that some of my most profound lessons came through the power of authenticity. The more I tried to fit the molds that were never meant for me, the more disconnected I had once felt. It was only when I embraced my own rhythm, my quirks, my scars, my distinct way of moving through the world, that I began living fully. Authenticity wasn't about perfection or performance; it was about alignment; allowing my actions, words, and dreams to reflect my true self. In choosing truth over approval, I not only found peace, but I also exuded quiet inspiration to others still searching for their own voice. Being true to myself had become my greatest act of freedom.

Appreciating and recognizing my own authenticity was something I learned through attrition. Being in situations that made me uncomfortable and out of place was common in my younger years. I bought into the idea that "fitting in" was of high importance. It took me years to realize that some of this mindset stems from insecurity and a lack of confidence. Although there are important aspects of community and acceptance, it is altogether another thing to hinge our self-worth on the chance that we are accepted into the "cool group." I had always felt like an outsider and a misfit compared to those cliques from high school and college, but now I actually embrace the differences between myself and "them." Part of this growth came from understanding that "they" didn't have it all together, either, and although on the surface they seemed to have it all figured out, they really were searching for something to make them feel better about themselves. Ultimately, we weren't all that different, but I recognized this and chose to be okay with the fact that I was on another course and needed to differentiate myself from the norm. I became more impressed with who I was becoming as a whole person and less impressed with the façade others were portraying. In fact, I giggle a bit now as I respectfully excuse myself from situations with "phony" people who are self-absorbed and condescending, and as I walk away, I make a point of whispering to myself, "I'm not impressed!"

I take things into my own hands these days because there is nobody more qualified to handle my life than myself! We sometimes view the words "accountability" and "responsibility" as concepts that represent criticism or negativity. They may even conjure up memories of being scolded in school or at home by an adult. However, perception is paramount when it comes to deconstructing the root cause of something in order to derive the benefits. If we are not accountable or responsible for our actions and lives, then who holds the power to make necessary changes for the better? Think about that for a moment; if we leave everything up to chance or fate, then where are we headed and what fixes our circumstances? Accepting responsibility and being accountable for ourselves is actually a very empowering and emboldened act on our own behalf. It places the power to steer our own course and make our own way, thus, providing the necessary capacity to get things done. Understanding the importance of taking things into my own hands has helped me immeasurably on my path to serving myself so I can serve others, too. I'm responsible, which means I am able/capable to dictate my responses, for my own actions because I'm the one driving the car, steering the ship, and I take accountability for my own life because it is the direct evidence of my power to evolve.

That little girl that was told she wasn't good enough, and wouldn't amount to much, finally graduated from medical school. Actually, I didn't just graduate, but I finished at the top of my class. The emotions still hit me as I type these words because it evokes so many memories, both good and rough, which eventually served me on my quest to become a doctor and purposeful person. I feel like I redeemed myself in many ways, but the most important thing to me is what I taught that younger version of myself; I reminded that little scared, unsure girl from back then of such wonderful life lessons through my progress. My eight-year-old self can breathe now and stand tall, while being comfortable in her own skin because of what "we" accomplished. Through myself, I know she's proud of herself and that brings me the most pride and joy. I will continue to make the younger version of myself proud as I inspire other women to be empowered and be the best they can be.

We are all works in progress, and we're learning along the way. How we progress and what we learn is essentially up to us, and we can find answers not only within books and through research of others, but also through the natural course of life, while we open our eyes, hearts, and minds to experiences. Our constant evolution is up to us, and we are at our best when we are free thinkers. There are so many exceptional experiences that await us, and we can fulfill our body, minds, and spirits through a life well lived if we are willing to go that extra distance. The naysayers will always be there, and the good, bad, and ugly will rear its head throughout the journey, but our world has so much to offer, and we possess the power to choose how we live our life. There's a famous line in the movie, The Shawshank Redemption spoken by Morgan Freeman's character: "Get busy livin' or get busy dyin." Our quality of life while we are here on Earth is entirely up to each of us, and the sooner we recognize the possibilities and take actionable steps toward a higher purpose, the sooner we can appreciate all the wonders of this world.

That truth would soon take physical form in my practice of stillness and movement. The next chapter of my journey would lead me to discover yoga, not as a trend or exercise, but as a reset ritual, a sacred meeting place between body and spirit. It became my way to reconnect when life grew loud, to release tension carried from the past, and to center myself amid the demands of medical school. What began as a few deep breaths on the mat would evolve into a lifelong discipline, one that reminded me, again and again, that strength and serenity could coexist within the same breath.

CHAPTER 8

"A Holistic Approach"

I became busy with my schooling and had little time for reflection, but when I looked back at some of the many obstacles that stood in my way, I decided to begin journaling. This simple decision helped me to understand not only what I was going through at certain times along my journey, but also how I solved some of those challenges. I became curious about the root causes of the anxiety I was experiencing at certain moments and scenarios. Although I chalked some of it up to the stressors of being a student in a high demanding field, I knew that there were some deep-seeded reasons that were getting in my way from time to time. For example, as I looked back at the anxiety attacks I had prior to taking my MCAT (Medical College Admissions Test) which prevented me from focusing and passing, I wondered where those fears were coming from and why were they being uprooted at such crucial moments in my journey.

Those words and the proclamations others spewed at me when I was young had me doubting myself during some of the most important school tests. A college professor even told me that I wasn't good enough because of my inability to manage my anxiety. Imagine that! A person in a key role in higher learning placing their stamp of negativity as if he were a judge sentencing my future, instead of offering constructive advice. These are people who are teaching medicine. It was astonishing to me, and it took me back to my childhood days of listening and internalizing the negative words from people who were larger than life influences on me. Fortunately, there were positive centers of influence during school as well; another professor shared some powerful words that would stay with me for the rest of my life. I remember him reminding me that he saw something in me that I may not have even known myself while emphasizing that not only was I good enough, but I was more than good enough to get into medical school and be an amazing doctor. Wow, his words helped to propel me to keep working toward my goal and to continue to focus on my strengths.

I knew I had to get past this, because if I didn't pass my MCAT, it would prevent me from moving on. As I reflect back, an old saying comes to mind that explains the choice when dealing with a major challenge or obstacle: we can look at the problem as a mountain that we can either go around or face and climb directly over it. Initial fear may urge us to take what seems like the easier route to go around, or even quit that path altogether. However, if we don't climb it, not only do we miss out on the journey and the view/experiences from getting up and over it, but we take a mental hit of regret that may rear its ugly head several times throughout our life.

I knew I had to get past my fears and climb that mountain directly. I decided to be proactive and see the school counselor. This simple act made a difference as the counselor assisted me, providing me with talk therapy and some basic tools. At the time though, I still felt a palpable sense of shame because it was almost frowned upon— as an admission of weakness, if you will, someone at this level of schooling to reach out for help. This sentiment was amplified when the regular primary doctor ran all the tests which were "normal" and he dismissed me and told me, "the stress was all in my head, here are some pills!" It was as if something was wrong with me. Again, the signs are apparent when it comes to how vicious cycles not only begin, but also perpetuate along the way, much like a small snowball that gains momentum until it becomes so big it's out of control and its new force is seemingly impossible to reverse. This was another life lesson for me as it was a strong reminder that, as a future doctor, I would not just follow the conventional path of medicine, but I would offer holistic, alternative ways of dealing with root causes for my patients, while showing empathy and compassion.

I came across yoga, which was a game changer for me. I met a yoga and meditation teacher on campus and joined a yoga club which was the beginning of my holistic journey. He trained in India, and I actually learned tools beyond the allopathic approach when it came to dealing with the anxiety that was impacting my ability to be in the right mindset to pass that all-important MCAT. It brought direct attention to the "bandage approach" whereby prescriptions are swiftly offered to those dealing with some of the challenges that can be mitigated through natural remedies. I learned about breath work and how to regulate my nervous system through yoga. I went out in nature on a trail right behind my apartment on campus, and that is where I'd get in touch and rebalance. This was so nurturing and nourishing for me not only within the visual sensations I was experiencing, but also in the neurological sense because it fed my mind with calm and serene fortifiers.

I began utilizing these visualization tools and was learning firsthand about the blending of eastern and western practices, not even realizing at the time that I would be able to create a movement and provide these tools to my future patients.

I continued to sharpen my holistic skills and honed my breath work, yoga, and visualizations. I was intrigued by these concepts and applications, and while I was learning the nuts and bolts of western medicine, I felt like I was also moonlighting in the field of eastern medicine. Just like that, a light bulb went off! I experienced an epiphany that revealed itself because I decided to climb that mountain and take in all the good, rough, and majestic roads. I became a seeker of answers as my whole world opened up to new possibilities. To me, there was more to medicine than what was written in a book or a prescription, and I was hooked on the idea of spreading the word to others. As I journaled, it occurred to me that I would have never learned any of the good things if I hadn't experienced some of the not-so-good things. If I hadn't struggled with some of that deep-seeded anxiety during my tests, I might never have sought out ways to deal with it—ways that led directly to my path of holistic and alternative medicine. We've talked about vicious cycles and their negative effects, but there are also "victorious cycles," and they have powerful and positive effects, too. This was certainly one for me.

I continued using these practices to get through all the challenges of undergrad, including taking the MCAT one more time, the fear of being rejected from medical school, and any obstacle I would face, and they worked! I passed, and I was able to get in. In fact, my interviewer at the University of Pikeville reminded me that, "What was outstanding wasn't just how you failed or fell down, and eventually made it, but the character and determination that kept you going—ultimately that was the most important thing. That is exactly what is needed to get into medical school, and that is what makes you truly different!" Wow, I was being commended for being different now in the most complimentary way. I thought about the irony of how I was once chastised in the past for not fitting in, but now at a prestigious level of education I'm being told that my uniqueness is one of my greatest strengths. That was such a valuable life lesson on perspective as nobody has the right to tell us what we can and can't do when it comes to our aspirations. We are all unique and beautiful in our own way, and although it is flattering and validating to hear compliments, it is even more important to empower ourselves with a positive self-image.

Even with my busy schedule, I still take the time to make entries into my journal today, and it helps me to not only reflect upon some of those key moments in my life, but it also reminds me how strong our minds are when we tap into some of the natural ways of self-improvement. We are fully capable of constantly learning, no matter what age or level we are at in life, and it begins with an open mind and an open heart. In some ways I'm grateful for having to experience the negative, derogatory, and inflammatory moments because it opened my eyes to how strong I was.

What began as personal practice soon evolved into something far greater. Yoga opened my eyes to a deeper understanding of energy, the kind that flows not only through movement, but through emotion, intention, and healing itself. The mat became more than a place of physical balance; it became a space of insight, where I learned that wellness was not confined to prescriptions or procedures, but rooted in harmony between mind, body, and spirit. As my awareness grew, so did my vision for the kind of doctor I wanted to become, one who would merge science with soul, structure with sensitivity. I began to study alternative modalities—meditation, breathwork, herbal support, and energy alignment, realizing that true healing wasn't just about treating symptoms but nurturing the whole person.

Medical education provided the tools of modern science, and I am certainly grateful for that knowledge, but yoga gave me the wisdom of ancient understanding. Integrating the two became my purpose: to create a bridge between evidence-based medicine and the subtle, restorative power of mindfulness and movement. Today I see in my clients what I had once seen in myself—fatigue, disconnection, and the yearning to be truly seen, not just diagnosed. And I know, deep within, that my calling is to help them return to balance, to show them that healing was never just physical, it was the art of reuniting the self.

Although I would never wish those early childhood experiences on anyone, I survived and eventually thrived despite them. If it wasn't for those times when I felt helpless and as if I was a failure, I might not have learned what I could overcome. The tough times ignited something in me, and they remind me to take the higher road in life and perpetuate good, healing practices for others who are looking for answers. Writing this book has been therapeutic as it's a continuation of my journaling and reflection, backed with the sincere hope that some of the "pillars of strength" outlined within will offer an empowering path for others.

CHAPTER 9

"Neuroplasticity & Rewiring"

Even as I grew more confident in my studies and purpose, anxiety still had its ways of creeping in. The pressure of exams, long shifts, and the emotional weight of caring for patients sometimes stirred a familiar restlessness in my chest, the same tightness I used to mistake for weakness. There were moments when doubt whispered louder than my conviction, when the old fears of not being enough resurfaced, dressed now in the language of medical precision and performance. Yet, instead of fighting against the unease, I learned to meet it, to pause, breathe, and look at it in the eye. I began to see anxiety not as an enemy, but as a messenger, a sign that I was growing beyond my comfort zone.

As simple as it may sound, breathing became my first line of response: slow, deep, deliberate inhales and exhales that calmed my nervous system and re-centered my focus. Meditation and mindful awareness followed, helping me to observe my emotions without being consumed by them. Over time, I began to sense how these tools didn't just ease anxiety, they strengthened my capacity to stay present, compassionate, and clear-headed, even in the most demanding situation.

It was through this practice, awareness, breath, and conscious rewiring that I continued to evolve, not just as a doctor, but as a healer in the truest sense.

There were times when it was difficult looking back at all the moments that caused me discomfort, stress, awkwardness, embarrassment, low self-worth, etc. I didn't know it at the time, but these were moments where I was experiencing anxiety in my life. Although I was getting through these difficult situations through resilience and even at times ignorance, they were taking a toll on me both physically and emotionally and would even boil over into panic attacks. The emotional manifestations of this trauma were playing out in a physical way that was damaging beyond my comprehension at the time. My later studies helped me to understand, process, and deal with this anxiety, and it has been such an eye-opening experience. The current version of myself wishes so badly she could help the younger, weaker, unsure, child version of myself. I couldn't go back in time to empower and uplift that girl, but I could look in the mirror and tell her, "I'm proud of you!" Also, through my medical and entrepreneurial work with others, including teaching my own children as a positive role model, I could make sure I would be part of the solution, not the problem.

In writing this book, I did a lot of reflection, and it has been a very therapeutic, and even at times uncomfortable experience because of the uprooting of some old wounds. Fortunately, I have the tools to dictate any negative outcome, while cutting off any triggers head on. Although I may be considered a cerebral person, I am also a very visual person, and as I wrote these words, I also had visions of their content through pictures in my mind. As I conveyed the important principles that served as cornerstones of my own healing, I envisioned pillars. Pillars are vital parts of any foundation and to me, this was the perfect example of what served as my support system.

Pillar #1= RECOGNITION

First and foremost is **recognition.** Again, this is where knowledge and empowerment come into play. Each of us has onset symptoms whereby we can detect and address our anxiety. For me, it was heart palpitations, followed by sweaty palms that left me feeling dizzy. Before I understood what this meant, fear set in which would spiral into a full-blown panic attack rendering me helpless. Like I mentioned before, I experienced such anxiety prior to my MCAT that I couldn't get through them, much less pass them. I didn't possess the arsenal that I do now that I needed to address, overcome, and eventually erase those anxious episodes. It's important not only to recognize when these anxious feelings are happening so you can offset them, but also understand your triggers and navigate different paths in order to divert yourself from specific situations that may be potentially provoking.

Pillar #2= ACTION/BREATHE

Although the phrase "knowledge is power" may seem a bit cliché' because its concept has been emphasized several times, it truly is the basis for any resolute plan of action. Now that you've recognized what is happening and why, let's put our knowledge to good use with our next pillar: Action through breath work. A great way to begin your plan of action is through counteraction! Utilizing your breathwork within the first 5 to 10 and even 30 seconds. In other words, "just breathe." This has proven to slow your heart rate, while providing necessary oxygen to the blood stream and even the brain. It might sound simple because breathing isn't something we usually have to think about, as it's a natural function of our miraculous body and mind. However, there are tools of breathing that promote not only physical manifestations, but also emotional manifestations, and these can be crucial in our overall well-being.

When we experience chronic stress, our breathing becomes shallow and fast, signaling to the brain that we're unsafe. Intentional breathwork retrains this pattern. By controlling the rhythm and depth of our breath, we can shift the body from "fight or flight" into "rest and repair." Two of the most effective, evidence-based techniques are the **4-7-8 breathing method and box breathing.** Each one activates the vagus nerve, lowers cortisol, and restores balance between the sympathetic and parasympathetic systems.

The 4-7-8 Breathing Technique

The 4-7-8 breath is designed to calm the nervous system, promote relaxation, and improve sleep quality. It's a gentle way to slow the heart rate and decrease stress response.

How to practice:

- Inhale slowly through your nose for **4 seconds.**

- Hold your breath for **7 seconds.**

- Exhale slowly and completely through your mouth for **8 seconds.**

Focus on deep belly breathing rather than chest breathing. This diaphragmatic movement stimulates the vagus nerve, the main communication line between your body and brain, and sends a powerful signal of safety to your nervous system.

The extended exhale helps to quiet the amygdala, reduce anxiety, and lower cortisol levels. It's an excellent technique to use before bed, after a stressful day, or anytime you need to regulate your emotions.

Box Breathing

Box Breathing, also known as four-square breathing, is a structured breath pattern that enhances focus, balance, and presence. It's often used by Navy SEALs and mindfulness practitioners to maintain calm under pressure.

How to practice:

- Inhale through your nose for 4 seconds.
- Hold your breath for 4 seconds.
- Exhale through your mouth for 4 seconds.
- Hold again for 4 seconds before repeating.

This equal pattern of breathing balances oxygen and carbon dioxide levels, stabilizes heart rate, and promotes mental clarity. Box breathing is particularly helpful before important meetings, during transitions, or in moments of overwhelm.

Both techniques are simple, free, and profoundly effective. Practiced consistently, they retrain the body to move from chronic stress toward calm, reminding your nervous system that you are safe, supported, and in control. As your breathing slows, your heart rate variability (HRV) improves—a key marker of resilience and stress recovery. Over time, consistent practice strengthens the vagus nerve, improves focus, and enhances emotional regulation. If you only remember one simple piece of advice, remember to breathe!

Pillar #3= NEUROPLASTICITY

I became fascinated with the science of neuroplasticity, and I understood that the brain, like the heart, could be rewired through intention and practice. Neuroplasticity in simple terms is the brain's ability to change and adapt throughout life. This is a fascinating phenomenon that is backed by science, and it is a wonderful reminder of how miraculous our bodies are, as well as how they work with our brain. With regard to anxiety, neuroplasticity can come into play as a natural defense mechanism, whereby the brain recognizes its structure and functions in response to experiences, learning, and trauma. Again, the pillar of recognition can be applied here. You might have heard of muscle memory, as this concept and application is commonly used within the sports world. For example, a basketball player practices shooting "free throws," and this action, over time, will be recognized by not only the brain, but our muscles/body. It can become an actual habit through the communication between our mind and body, as our muscles through repeated bodily movement/motion recognize the act of shooting the ball from that specific distance. When we learn something new, our brain sends messages between neurons, and if we repeat this action enough times, our brain creates a connection between the neurons. We've all heard the phrase "practice makes perfect;" well, now we know why.

We can teach our mind and body not only how to cope with anxiety and trauma, but also how to pivot from one perspective to another, while mitigating triggers, and even change our brain chemistry through neuroplasticity. "Neuro" is the defining word used when discussing the brain, and "plasticity" means: the quality of being easily shaped or molded. When broken down and visualized, the seemingly intimidating word "neuroplasticity" becomes our friendly ally. Entire books are written about this phenomenon, as well as many case studies, but for the sake of efficiency, let's discuss neuroplasticity within the context of coping with anxiety for now.

Imagine creating new neural pathways within your brain that can offset your anxiety. It's possible to build neural pathways that promote calmness and confidence by giving your brain an alternative response. We can delve deep within the science of neuroplasticity, neurons, epigenetics, etc. Because there is so much information about this subject, and although it may seem a bit confusing at first, you may find yourself fascinated by it and even surprised that you may be practicing it already. There are some simple exercises like meditation, learning a new skill, changing thought patterns, physical exercise, and even doing some challenging brain activity like crossword puzzles that stimulate neuroplasticity. These activities can help promote calmness, mental clarity and perspective, all while reducing stress and anxiety.

Getting to know the root cause of your anxiety, triggers, and responses is just as important as learning ways to overcome these challenges. We know "what" happens during the anxious moments (anxiety/panic attacks) in our lives, but we should also take the time to understand the "why" and "how," as well. Learning more about your body can teach you why you're experiencing such challenges and how to overcome them. The more we understand ourselves within, the more we can teach ourselves new pathways. If we take the time to empower ourselves with the essential information, we can redefine who we are, where we're going, and how we will arrive there.

I like using the concept of a bridge as an analogy when talking about dealing with anxiety and creating new stimuli for overcoming challenging moments. Picture a beautiful plush area that is filled with fruit trees that you are trying to reach, but this land is surrounded by a rushing river and steep terrain. You need to get to the other side in order get that fruit, but the fear sets in every time you look at those trees because of the dangerous conditions that surround them, so you give up on the idea by avoiding it altogether. What if you could build a bridge to arrive there safely? In other words, you can create different pathways to attain a desired result. Imagine how different and difficult our world would be without bridges. Imagine how much better our world is with bridges, and how much better we could connect with others through bridging the gaps we have between us, too. We can build bridges within our mind that can create a better path, which not only relieve and possibly relinquish our anxieties, but also provide a whole new perspective in how we see ourselves, our world, and each other.

CHAPTER 10

"On Purpose"

As I share some of my experiences that served as pillars of strength and growth, both in this book and through my entrepreneurial endeavors, I'm reminded of the blessings of gratitude I feel within the depths of my heart and soul. Had it not been for some of the good, challenging, and even painful experiences along the way, I might not have had the opportunity to realize the joys of this wonderful journey we call life. One of the things that brings me great pleasure is sharing insights and information with others, in the hope that they may find their own path less daunting and more fulfilling. Through authenticity, purpose, and recalibration, we can create a more balanced experience along the way, while in pursuit of our endeavors.

There comes a point in every journey when you must pause, breathe, and recalibrate. Life has a way of pulling us off course, into comparison, expectation, or the noise of what others think we should be. But the true work lies in returning to authenticity, in remembering who you are beneath all the layers, beyond the limitations the world tries to place upon you. Being on purpose isn't about constant motion;

it's about conscious direction—choosing each step with clarity, integrity, and heart. It's a reminder that alignment matters more than speed, and that when your actions flow from your truth, everything else begins to fall into place. This chapter is a call to realignment—to slow down, breathe deeply, and live each day with intention so your purpose can move through you, not just around you.

BE AUTHENTIC

I remember struggling with this concept because of those feelings of insecurity and lack of self-worth at a young age. Without encouragement and support from early on, I not only questioned who I was, but also if I was even capable and worthy of some of the blessings I saw in others. I began to think I didn't deserve good things because of what and who I was told I was. Children are prone to conditioning from the negative things they see and hear. If exposed to this often enough, it becomes engrained in their mindset, thus fulfilling that narrative. Fortunately, this goes for exposure to positive reinforcement factors, as well. Although I didn't have such nurturing early influences, I recognized through trial and error that I was a valuable person and eventually received enough validating words and milestones that I drew upon for momentum.

Some are fortunate enough to realize that they can become their best versions of themselves, regardless of what others think and/or say about them. It took me years to realize that being and becoming my authentic self was more than good enough. I accepted myself for who I was organically and worked hard on complimenting my strengths, while working on my weaknesses. It is my mission to help others realize that they can achieve great things, all while staying true to their authentic self.

I truly believe we come into this world with gifts to share with ourselves and others. We all have inherent and entrusted blessings that, once discovered, can be put to positive use, backed by purpose, while impacting those we meet along the way. At some point in my early years, I felt out of place and thought it best to conform or fly under the radar altogether. When we choose to become a version of ourselves that's meant to fit in, or just to be accepted, while not staying true to who we are, we simply stunt our growth, and instead of evolving into our potential, we move further from who and what we're meant to be. In the process, we deny ourselves and the world of our gifts.

Often times, the nature of who we are may go unnoticed, unrealized, and even lost over time. We've all heard the phrases "end of the innocence," and "the good old days," or know someone who became bitter with age. These are examples of allowing life and conditions around us to dictate who we become, while looking through a darkened lens. Negativity doesn't have to be our default! We have the choice to be our authentic selves and thrive in the skin we're in. Yes, there will be reasons and situations that tempt us to pull toward the side of pessimism, and it can become easy to fall into that trap, but being aware that we are the artist, sculptor and designer of our own self and, then creating the masterpiece with our already beautiful clay, landscape, and canvas, can be both empowering and refreshing.

Be proud of who you are already within your nature and work toward enhancing that person along the way. "Finding myself" can be an admission and first step that we are aware of a deeper understanding of who we are with a "return to me" type of approach. Oftentimes, this recognition is effective because we're acknowledging that we may have drifted off course from our organic roots.

This is where our next pillar can guide us back on the right track, while maintaining the integrity of our natural origins.

RECALIBRATION

Defined in the Merriam Webster Dictionary, recalibration means: to make small changes to an instrument so that it measures accurately. This certainly applies as literal representation of what we're talking about with regard to our body, mind, and spirit being the instrument that can be finely tuned in order to fulfill our potential and create balanced living. First, there must be recognition that changing/finely-tuning is necessary for improvement. The popular catch phrase "best version of ourselves" can often sound familiar, especially in a self-improvement setting, and while most of us may be striving to do just that, we mustn't forget to stay true to ourselves while we make these small adjustments. Furthermore, the value of added balance should be part and parcel of the process. The ultimate goal is to create an effective, fulfilling, and harmonious environment inwardly so that we can manifest our experiences outwardly.

Another version of the concept of recalibration can be found within the online website www.dictionary.com: To reexamine (one's thinking, a plan, a system of values, etc.) and correct it in accord with a new understanding or purpose. This explanation accurately reflects a more specific idea of self-improvement. You may notice that these actions are very much aligned with another pillar, which is Self-Care. Implementing a morning routine, for example, can do wonders for not only getting started on the right path daily, but can also provide the very balance that can carry us through the day.

There are going to be stressors facing us daily, both personally and professionally. Whether you're single or married within a family dynamic, along with kids, there are responsibilities, accountability, and let's be frank—stress! There are tasks both professionally and personally that require action, which can cause anxiety and apprehension. This not only can wear on the mind, but also the body, thus fueling a counter-productive outcome. Remember our pillar reminding us to breathe? This would be a good time to do just that, then create a plan of action within a routine that not only offsets any future chaos, but also provides perspective which turns a "problem" into a conquerable challenge. Remember that mountain that looks so formidable? With a routine that recalibrates us, it now becomes a beautiful monument of opportunity to climb, while appreciating the experience along the way.

Yoga, meditation, prayer, reading, journaling, etc., are all examples of recalibration activities. Whichever works best for you is the answer that is best for you. Use your imagination and find what is the most effective and personalized option for yourself. Often, a combination of several of these tools can have an immediate and positive impact on us. Music is another great way to feed the soul. Do you have a memorable song that evokes joy when you hear it? Turn it on and turn it up! Sound healing, for example, sound bowls and binaural beats can adjust your brain waves from a chaotic state to a calm state. Music is enjoyable for many reasons, but it goes well beyond the surface of enjoyment, there are physiological effects that are good for us when we listen to music. Dopamine release can be triggered in many ways that can serve us well. Nature answers the call when we invite her in with music, exercise, sunlight, social interaction, meditation, sleep, healthy diet, and many other simple and pleasurable activities. Take that walk and notice this beautiful place we get to call home. There is beauty all around us and beauty within us and when we are aware and living in the present, while emitting the energy of kindness and joy, it becomes contagious!

BE ON PURPOSE

"Find your gift, then share it with others," is a paraphrased version of a quote that is inspired by: "The purpose of life is to find your gift, and the meaning of life is to give it away!" (Often attributed to Pablo Picasso). The moral messages are the same. While on this journey, it is my personal belief that there are inherent gifts that have been bestowed upon us which are unique to each of us and our place in this world. Some people are natural caregivers, teachers, artists, entertainers, entrepreneurs, scientists, innovators, etc. and these can translate into several complimentary fields. These attributes may be more noticeable for some, while others must seek them out. Either way, with an open mind and open heart, they will be revealed.

Once we find our gift/purpose and decide to pursue a path that best highlights our talents, we can then ask ourselves "What is my why?" In other words, "What is my driving force?"—the reason behind why I do what I do. Whatever your answer to this question is—will most likely reveal the meaning behind why you do it. When we are living on purpose, many of the forces are in place, especially good karmic energy, including helping others with acts of kindness, generosity, empathy, and compassion.

With our world seemingly moving faster than ever, it can be challenging to take the time out of our busy lives to make sure our purpose is in alignment with positive values. However, I have found that not only can we balance a career and family life with a positively fulfilling and impactful experience, but oftentimes when we are doing something that helps others, momentum and success actually become our ally.

Throughout my journey as a doctor, I made a conscious decision to be different in my approach while working with patients. Through my own trials and tribulations, I became compassionate and empathetic toward others. Part of this was my natural gift I was born with, and some was learned through what I yearned for in my experiences. I remembered that little girl in me who needed so badly to feel supported and validated, and I believe this translated into my bold decision to make sure that I was part of the solution and not the problem when it came to caregiving, teaching, speaking, and parenting. I wanted to remind others of their value and how they can better live a fulfilling and empowered life. I enjoy helping others, and this has become the meaning of life for me, which includes one of the greatest joys: being a mom to my two children. If we are living on purpose while pursuing our endeavors, then it definitely becomes a win-win!

Whether speaking to groups of women or a mix of people from all walks of life, it gives me great pleasure to not only share my story, but also provide insights that can help embolden others. I want nothing more than to be an example of what is possible, and how the pillars outlined in this book have helped me live a purposeful life, while maintaining a healthy balance. Knowledge is power, and when we share with others through purpose and kindness, we create a cycle of goodness that benefits all.

CHAPTER 11

"Why Not?"

Every great transformation begins with baby steps, the quiet, consistent choices that slowly carve a new path. It's easy to wait for the perfect moment, the clear sign, the guarantee that everything will work out. But life has a way of teaching clarity after the leap, not before it. Each time I chose to trust myself, even in small ways, I chipped away at the barriers of fear and doubt. I began to change the cycles of being a victim by asking a different question of "why not me?" instead of the habitual, "why me?" Why not believe I could build something extraordinary from the very pieces that once held me back? That shift, from hesitation to possibility became the spark that guided me through every new challenge and opportunity ahead.

When we open ourselves to possibility instead of anticipating obstacles, something changes within us. There's a chemistry that happens, a kind of alchemy between faith and action. The body softens, the mind expands, and the spirit begins to hum with quiet anticipation. Suddenly, doors we never noticed start to appear, and the right people, ideas, and experiences begin to align as if summoned by our readiness. I began to feel that energy often, the current of creation that moves when we stop resisting and start receiving. Possibility, I discovered, isn't luck or magic. It's chemistry, the natural reaction that occurs when courage meets openness, and when we finally allow life to rise and meet halfway.

While writing this book to share with others, I was blessed with a therapeutic experience that allowed me to reminisce about the path that little girl had taken. In a way, as I began to articulate the many challenges and milestones along my journey, I realized there were some visuals that truly helped me, and I certainly hope they will be of great purpose to you as well. Although I knew little or nothing about visualization at the time, I did have an imagination that often had me seeing myself in certain scenarios. As I look back, I can picture a hillside which offered several ways to cross over; there was a well-beaten path that represented the trodden journey of my ancestors who had less choices than I, or at the very least, were conditioned to take that same route. While this was a proven way to reach the other side, it offered very little in the way of experiencing unique and joyful sights along the way. I knew this was not the path for me as it offered little in the way of fulfillment.

There was also an unknown route that was blurred by dense fog on one side, but in the distance on the other side was the ocean and a glimmer of the city lights. I was intrigued by this path as I knew there would be some unknown adventures along the way. While it might prove to be a bit more challenging route, there was that beautiful body of water that stretched toward a lively scene which piqued my curiosity. This route gave me hope that there was something exciting out there. I began to walk.

Among the other options was a longer path that was strewn with beautiful flowers and trees that were separated by craggy rocks and rushing streams. I was drawn to its beauty and intrigued by its appeal, and yet a little fearful to navigate its offering. I took a few steps in its direction to see what lay ahead. All of the paths shared some common themes—they all had some rough terrain in their own way, they all led to another side, and there was likely to be different vantage points along the way. The differences that became obvious were two-fold: the more beaten path offered little in the way of life as there was no growth around it, with less beauty than the others, and it was certainly a less colorful route. The other options would bring a sense of challenge, exuberance, and beauty, as well as a little of the unknown.

As I looked beyond what seemed like a hard decision to make, I realized one outstanding thing: I got to choose my path. Even if some of the trails led me a bit astray, I could venture over to include parts of the other trails. Moreover, I could even carve my own path, which inspired me greatly. The bottom line was that there are options out there, and they can be uniquely customized to your gifts. Sometimes the answers aren't fully clear in regard to what road will lead you where you want to go, but part of the beauty is figuring it out. Whether the vision includes natural scenery, a beautiful structure that is stabilized by strong pillars, or an image that pops up in your psyche during a deep meditative state, it's all about being open to the possibilities.

If you should have but one broad takeaway from this book, it is my hope that you realize your power to choose your own path. Of course, there will be challenges along the way because that is life. Besides, how boring would it be if there wasn't an obstacle or two that forces us into some growth? But there are so many things that are truly miraculous in this life that we can experience, and it's available to us. We are the creator of our own journey, and the sooner we realize that we do, indeed, control our destiny, the sooner we can begin consuming this adventure with an open heart and open mind.

The very common denominator that saved me from the path that would lead me through another vicious cycle and chalk me up as another casualty, was the realization that I could pull my own strings and did not have to be the puppet. I'm so very thankful that this came to me in time to save me. Maybe it was whispered by the many voices of women through the generations who couldn't speak up in their own lifetimes. Or maybe it was a rebellious spirit that already existed within. I'm not sure, but I'm glad I heeded their calls and cries for help. I can unequivocally attribute most of this awareness through knowledge. I was blessed by geography, as I was living in a free country, which opened my eyes to opportunities. I am grateful to my parents, who knew life in America came with certain opportunities that their native countries did not have, especially at the time. Also, I knew I despised the idea of being trapped in a life that others had dictated for me. All the noise I heard around me made it clear that although sometimes people were rooting against me, I felt that the universe was an open canvas and available to me. I remember a saying I heard at a network event: "The universe is conspiring to help me." This idea is polar opposite to those who feel they have "bad luck" or a "black cloud" over them. It's important that we manifest positive thoughts and possibilities as our mind is so powerful that it will feed on either negativity, which stunts and shuts down, or positivity, which will blossom innovation and possibilities. I visualized what was possible and placed myself in scenarios within my mind of where I would be in five, ten, and twenty years.

What happens when we shift from asking ourselves why things are the way they are in our lives and the world in general to an even more powerful question: "Why not?" Our mind is a miraculous thing that is fed not only through actions/stimuli, but also what it is being told. In other words, if we feed it with "Why?" or "I can't," it can easily be shut down to the possibilities. Whereas a "Why not?" or "I can" keeps the door open to begin taking action toward a goal. We've talked about the power of neuroplasticity and creating a sort of muscle memory which can transform entire belief systems. Our body, mind, and spirit are gifts and, to an extent, largely untapped resources. Find that inner power within by slowing down, breathing, and visualizing a more prosperous, peaceful, joyful path.

I heard the words "no," "can't," and "never" a lot in my youth, and I saw how it broke down so many others along the way. Like many things, negativity, too, is a habit, and there is such a sense of hopelessness to this cyclical way of thinking. It is perpetuated through generations, and it is simply toxic. How about saying yes to the possibilities? Yes to your peace of mind. Yes to your purpose. Yes to your wellness, and yes to whatever it is that will complement the already miraculous being that you are! Maybe your situation is different; maybe you're already ahead of where I had to start, or you are even in tougher circumstances. Understand that progress is within your grasp, no matter what your place is in this world.

Begin with baby steps as you build a foundation while using your pillars of strength. It won't happen overnight, but it will happen. Start creating your strongest structure, and you will not only realize the very best this life has to offer, but you'll be equipped with tools from within so that you'll enjoy the ride, not just the destination. Your body, mind, and spirit are truly unique, and the path is yours to make, take, and appreciate. Life doesn't have to be a series of arduous struggles, or an unfulfilling existence. You have purpose, and you have the power to build it the way you want it.

Visualization is a vital part of the process of creating change. Acknowledging your situation by either circumstance or choice allows you to create a plan of action through what you see in your mind's eye. Imagination is not just for the young, neither is daydreaming. Your current position is your reality—recognize that it will soon become your past through a series of movements toward your goal and a reminder that you are, indeed, in control. If accountability isn't realized, then who holds the power to make a difference? If you allow outside influences to pull your strings, you will be stagnant as you wait for others. Whether your situation is a result of cards you've been dealt or a series of choices you made or did not make isn't as material as your next action now! You are in charge! You are empowered! You are gifted, and it is up to you and only you to sculpt your very best life! Start by picturing yourself within the scenery of your new and improved life setting, and you'll be on your way of becoming whatever it is that you visualize. Along the way, it is my hope that you remember to take the time to enjoy the scenery.

CHAPTER 12

"Imagine"

Like I've mentioned throughout this book, we are all "works in progress," and by no means, is there a quick fix, exact science, or even a guidebook that holds all the answers to our ever-evolving individual lives. However, there exists, now more than ever, information readily available that can provide us with the pearls of wisdom to enhance our experience while on this journey. Often, there have been moments in my own life that had me doubting many things. You may be experiencing some challenges that you're not quite sure how to navigate and overcome. I'm grateful that I can now see beyond my current situation and remain hopeful that not only will things get better, but I now have the tools to embrace the moment while tapping into my wherewithal to live in the present, no matter what I am facing. In fact, if there is one thing I am hopeful for as you read this book, it is that you become more hopeful in your daily life. "Hope is a good thing, maybe the best of things, and no good thing ever dies." **(The Shawshank Redemption).**

None of us are finished; we are constantly being shaped, softened, and strengthened by life's unseen hands. There is no final version of perfection, only growth, grace, and gratitude. Every sunrise, every unexpected kindness, every breath is a quiet miracle reminding us that life itself is sacred. And perhaps the greatest miracle of all is the simple fact that we are here, learning, evolving, loving, daring to begin again, one imperfect and beautiful step at a time.

Also, I hope you are reminded of the fact that you are not alone, no matter how alone you may sometimes feel. Even while writing this book, I experienced some push back by a small few from whom I expected support and encouragement. During growth periods of your life, you may notice that the circle of people you expected to draw strength and support from, is changing and rearing its ugly head. It happens, and it may be rooted not only in jealousy, but also in fear because your growth has illuminated their lack of progress in their own lives. Progress by some is a threat to others at times and unfortunately, it's become more prevalent, or at least more obvious because of increased lines of communication. Our human default, especially on social media, has become one of critique and scorn. It is imperative to understand that what others do or say in the light of your growth, is their evolution (or lack thereof), not yours. You can remain diligent, respectful, and laser focused on your path, all while staying true to yourself and those most important to you. I'm ultimately responsible for myself and my children's well-being, and I've learned, the hard way at times, that I can't allow others to trigger the stunting of my growth (nor should you), even if it comes from family, a spouse, or a friend.

Each pillar is similar to the links in a chain as they rely on each other for overall strength. This book was meant to be a reference guide, too, so just like a journal, please go back and call upon the information that you may need at certain points along your journey. While busy with everyday life, it can become easy to lose focus or even fall off track once in a while, so it's super important to remain diligent about following a healthy routine until it becomes habit. Waking up with gratitude is something I remind myself about every morning. I'm thankful for this day I've been blessed with and excited to hug my children, and I become mentally prepared to address my day. Drinking water first thing in the morning helps to awaken my organs, and breathing exercises take only a minute or two to ease my mind and calm my heart. Depending on my schedule, I'll either do my stretching in the morning or evening, or both, but this is important to me because my muscles need it, as well as my mind. Stretch your mind by keeping it open to possibilities, and stretch your body, and you'll notice the dividends. Flexibility in your daily life is crucial, both literally and figuratively.

As I look back at that little girl I once was, I visualize myself looking into the mirror and realizing the transformation from pain to empowerment. I wish things could have been different for that younger version of me, especially in those vulnerable years, but I'm super proud of how we developed. It took a lot of intestinal fortitude to face those challenges, and even though I grew stronger with each milestone I overcame, there is still a part of me that is driven to avenge the hurt that my younger self experienced. However, instead of dwelling on the pain, I now pay homage to that little girl by living in gratitude and leading by example, with an empowering voice and compassionate mindset. These days I have learned to channel those thoughts into positive outcomes not only for myself, but also my clients, patients, and those around me. There is a light within us all, and we have choices that we can make to shine that light for ourselves, as well as those who may need it as a beacon of hope.

I may not have noticed or even understood at the time, but I was reminded time and again that the imagination is one of our greatest forms of power. It is where vision is born, where healing begins, and where the seeds of change first take root. Everything that ever existed, every breakthrough, every new beginning, lived as a quiet thought in someone's mind. To imagine is to believe in what is not yet visible; it is to invite the future into the present moment. It's important to protect your imagination, to feed it with wonder instead of worry, knowing that the stories we tell ourselves become the lives we live. Imagination, I realize, is not escapism, it's the blueprint of creation.

One of the key pillars that you won't read in most personal development books is the importance of **Imagination.**

It's usually something discussed regarding childhood or within the art/creative world, but not much emphasis is placed on it as an integral part of our development. I was fortunate enough to have a healthy imagination from an early age, and it was my imagination that painted a picture of hope for me. Yes, after I achieved a milestone or beat the odds to overcome a difficult obstacle, I certainly gained momentum and strength that gave me the confidence to keep going but it started because I imagined a better way. I saw the possibilities, instead of the impossibilities. I was a daydreamer, and that is something that should be embraced within our children and our own inner child. Because not only does our imagination stoke something very creative within us, it can also provide a glimpse into what could be, which will evoke feelings of being in that particular setting. There will always be noise around us, even those who will constantly say, "You can't," but a healthy imagination, backed by purpose and action, can be an integral part of our growth and mindset. It was my imagination that helped manifest my future. I visualized myself making the basketball team, and I dreamt of taking a different path, like the time I joined the military. Even though it shocked a lot of people, it didn't shock me, because I had already imagined it. I pictured myself helping others as a doctor in ways that were very personal and important to me.

Life is precious! I think we can all agree on this, and there are reminders, both beautiful and daunting, of this throughout our journey. Life and death are still mysterious in ways we may never fully understand. Still, we can truly embrace the miracle of life even when things don't go our way. The magic is in the realization that we are here for a reason, and we can put this reason to good use. While there are fears and outcomes that don't always serve us in the moment, we can certainly grow from life lessons if we stay open to the possibilities and remind ourselves that our time here is finite. What we do with this time is ultimately up to us, regardless of obstacles and the cards we're dealt. We can't control everything, of course, but we can control what we're going to invest in while we are breathing and our heart is beating.

One doesn't have to look too far to witness the miracle of life, especially if you've seen the birth of a child and/or the development of a baby within a woman's womb via sonogram. Millions of things have to happen for this all to occur, and the timing is meticulous, like the most unbelievable and resilient machine. We come into this world as miracles, and we remain miracles every single day. Sometimes, we forget this and lose track of the fact that we are miraculous. We are miracles at work within this epic galaxy that has no end or beginning, living on a planet that is seemingly suspended within nothingness. As far as we know, the conditions elsewhere are uninhabitable (at least for now), so why don't we value ourselves more? Why don't we value the lives of our fellow humans more? Maybe we fall off track and get caught up in the day-to-day grind and lose sight of who and what we really are, and are meant to be.

Why is it that we are here at this particular time in history, and what are we supposed to be doing with the finite amount of time we have been blessed with? I certainly don't have all the answers; most of us don't. However, I am a true believer that we are blessed with certain gifts, and these gifts are to be discovered by ourselves through an open mind and open heart. Then we are to share these gifts with others. We can do this with our children of course, because we innately want the very best experience for them during their journey. But we can also do it with others, as well as within our career. It doesn't have to be restricted to monetary gifts or grand gestures of philanthropy either, often a listening ear, a cup of coffee, a moment shared, a phone call, a text, or any reminder to others (and ourselves) that we are in this together and all worthy of love.

I'm grateful every single day that I'm able to positively affect the health and wellness of others. But it doesn't take a vocation to have a positive impact on others, as we can all contribute to people by sharing just a smile, a kind gesture, or perhaps a positive word. We can be consciously aware of a higher purpose for the betterment of our fellow beings in ways that can reverberate throughout society. Become aware of the very fact that you are not only the difference maker in your own life, but you can also help lift up others to do the same and pay it forward. It starts with you and how you treat yourself, your energy, and those around you, and you'll experience joy in ways you might never have thought possible. I wish you well on your journey, and I'm truly grateful you allowed me to share mine with you. Remember, no matter where you come from, or what others may tell you, always remember you were born a miracle and you are a light meant to shine in this world, and you already possess the power of choice. Use this power wisely and create your best life possible. Begin building your well-balanced foundation—pillar by pillar!

Empowerment Tools Inspired

by Dr. Remina Panjwani's Book Journey

Introduction

This supplemental guide was created to enrich your experience with Dr. Remina Panjwani's book. As a veteran, physician, and holistic wellness advocate, Dr. R. shares not only her life story but valuable tools to help others break generation cycles, build self-worth, and cultivate mental, physical, and spiritual resilience. This guide includes science-backed practices and self-reflection prompts inspired by each chapter

Chapter by Chapter Tools & Insights

Chapter 1: Overcoming Cultural Conditioning

Tool: Inner Child Dialogue

- Write a letter to your younger self affirming your worth.
- Recognize negative inherited beliefs and write down how you'd reframe them today

Science Insight: Adverse childhood experiences (ACE) shape neural wiring. Positive reparenting through self-dialogue can reduce amygdala hyperactivity and promote resilience.

Chapter 2: Belonging Through Self-Discovery

Tool: Identity Anchoring

- Create a "strengths list" from moments you felt unique, capable, or brave.
- Ask: "What did I enjoy that others didn't? How can I lean into that today?"

Science Insight: Dopaminergic reward pathways are activated when we pursue intrinsic interests, reinforcing self-directed behavior.

Chapter 3: Fueling Growth with Doubt

Tool: Turn Criticism into Fuel

- Create a "Prove Them Wrong" journal. Document every moment where you've defied expectations.
- Set one challenge per week that reminds you of your power.

Science Insight: Self-efficacy builds with small wins. Consistent exposure to manageable challenges boosts prefrontal cortex control over fear-based responses.

Chapter 4: Breaking Vicious Cycles

Tool: Vicious-to Victorious Mapping

- Draw two columns: One for inherited patterns (e.g. silence, burnout), one for your new choices (e.g. voice, boundaries).
- Commit to one replacement action per week.

Mantra: *"I'm possible!"*

Science Insight: Epigenetic research shows we can silence stress-reactive genes with consistent wellness practices.

Chapter 5: Education as Liberation

Tool: Personal Development Plan

- Choose one skill to learn that aligns with your future self.
- Break it into micro-goals.

Science Insight: Lifelong learning maintains hippocampal volume and delays cognitive decline.

Chapter 6: The Pillars of Strength

Tool: The Pillars Practice

Each week: focus on one of the following pillars:

- **Open-mindedness:** Try something unfamiliar.
- **Breathwork:** 5-10 minutes of box breathing daily (4 in, 4 hold, 4 out, 4 hold)
- **Nourishment:** Aim for 1.2 – 1.6 g/kg of protein per pound of body weight daily depending on your activity level. Prioritize complete proteins (chicken, fish, eggs, legumes + grains, tofu, etc.).
- Focus on **blood sugar stability** by including protein, fiber, and healthy fats in each meal.
- Stay hydrated: **Drink half your body weight in ounces of water daily** (e.g. 150 lbs. = 75 oz).

- **Eat the rainbow:** Include a variety of colorful fruits and vegetables to ensure micronutrient diversity.
- **Limit processed foods** and refined sugars, which contribute to inflammation and mood swings.
- Track your **food & mood** for 7 days to identify how specific foods affect your energy, focus, and digestion.
- **Self-Care:** Book one appointment that's only for your well-being.

Science Insight: Breath regulation activates the vagus nerve, shifting the nervous system from sympathetic (fight/flight) to parasympathetic (rest/digest). Protein helps stabilize neurotransmitter production (e.g. tryptophan ~ serotonin) and supports muscle and hormone repair.

Chapter 7: Authentic Empowerment

Tool: Inner CEO Exercise

- Sit quietly and ask: "What do I want ?"
- Write out an authentic YES or NO for your life.

Science Insight: Self-authorship is linked to greater life satisfaction and agency, especially among marginalized groups.

Chapter 8: Yoga, Therapy & The Nervous System

Tool: Daily Reset Ritual

- 10-minute yoga Nidra or breath-based meditation.
- Journal one moment of calm daily.

Science Insight: Yoga and meditation increase GABA levels, reducing anxiety and improving focus.

Chapter 9: Neuroplasticity & Rewiring

Tool: Trigger Rewire Protocol

- **Recognition:** Notice the trigger.
- **Breathe:** 3 deep breaths.
- **Reframe:** "What's a new way to see this?"

Science Insight: Each time you direct a thought pattern, you reinforce new neural pathways. Neuroplasticity favors repetition.

Chapter 10: Living on Purpose

Tool: Purpose Audit

- List 3 things that make you lose track of time (flow).
- How can these become more present in your week?

Science Insight: Purpose-driven individuals have lower cortisol levels and increased NK (natural killer) cell activity, improving immune health.

Chapter 11: Choosing Your Path

Tool: Fog to Focus Map

- Write one decision you've avoided.
- Under "fog": What's unclear? What are you afraid of?"
- Under "focus: "What's true? What are your values?"
- Take one small step today.

Mantra: *"Why not me?"*

Science Insight: Decision-making aligned with values reduces anxiety and improves long-term satisfaction (self-determination theory).

Chapter 12: The Power of Imagination and Miracles

Theme: Becoming the Architect of Your Future

Tool: The Imagination Practice

- Spend 5 minutes each morning visualizing your ideal self or day.
- What does your energy feel like?
- What are you surrounded by?
- What impact are you making?
- Write down one inspired action that moves you closer to that vision
- End your visualization with the affirmation: **"I am a miracle in motion, creating my life through purpose and imagination."**

Tool: The Gratitude Activation Routine

- Upon waking, place your hand over your heart and list three things you are grateful for, one about your body, one about your life, and one about someone else.
- Drink a full glass of water while taking three slow, deep breaths.
- Stretch your body gently and visualize light expanding through your spine.
- Remind yourself: "I am flexible in body, mind, and life."

Tool: Protect Your Imagination

- Limit exposure to negativity (especially online) that dims your creative spirit.
- Replace self-doubt with curiosity. Ask: *"What if it all works out?"*
- Keep an "Imagination Journal" where you write your visions, ideas, and intuitive nudges no matter how unrealistic they may seem.

Science Insight:

Neuroscience confirms that imagination activates the same neural circuits as actual **experience.** Visualization increases motivation, enhances motor performance, and even alters gen expression related to stress and growth. Functional MRI scans show that imagining success fires the same neurons used when physically performing the action—training the brain for future achievement.

Holistic Insight:

Imagination is not escapism; it's a bridge between the unseen and the possible. When combined with emotional alignment (gratitude, calm, and hope), imagination becomes a form of energetic manifestation, influencing both neurochemistry and behavior.

Reflection Prompts:

- When have I used imagination to overcome fear or limitation?
- How can I protect and nourish my creative mind daily?
- What miracle have I witnessed~ in myself or others~ that reminds me of life's sacredness?

Mantra: *"Imagination is the birthplace of transformation."*

Integration Practice:

Before bed, close your eyes and imagine your highest future self—healthy, abundant, peaceful, and fulfilled. Breathe deeply and let your body feel the emotions of that version of you. Repeat nightly. Your brain will begin wiring this as your default state.

Science Insight~ The Miracle of You:

From a biological perspective, the odds of your existence are estimated at 1 in 400 trillion. Every heartbeat, cellular renewal, and conscious breath is proof that you are a living miracle. Recognizing this truth enhances serotonin and oxytocin release—hormones tied to connection, joy, and meaning.

Final Reflections

This guide is your invitation to rewrite your narrative. Like Dr. Remina, you have the power to transform ancestral patterns, access your authenticity, and thrive in your own design.

Share your reflections on your social media using #ImPossible #RewriteYourStory #EmpoweredByDrR

Want More?

Connect with Dr. Remina for upcoming wellness programs, holistic retreats, and mentorship opportunities:

You are your greatest project. Start building!

ABOUT THE AUTHOR

Driven by both passion and compassion, Dr. Remina Panjwani continues to inspire others to redefine wellness on their own terms. She stands as a living reminder that healing begins from within, and that with courage, intention, and heart—transformation is always possible. A devoted mother of two, an entrepreneur, empowerment champion, and a dedicated healer, Dr. Remina Panjwani will continue to use her voice and knowledge for the betterment of others.

After years in traditional medicine, Dr. Remina Panjwani noticed an unsettling pattern: some of the very professionals entrusted with healing others themselves were burned out, exhausted, and feeling disconnected within a hectic system. Witnessing this widespread imbalance became a turning point, a precipice that inspired her to reimagine healthcare altogether.

Through her own personal and professional evolution, she embraced a more holistic, integrative approach—one that honors both science and soul, data and intuition. This realization led her to establish "Optimizing Wellness Together," a wellness-focused practice built on compassion, empowerment, and conscious care. Her mission is simple yet profound: to guide others toward true well-being, not just the absence of illness, but the presence of vitality, peace, and purpose.

If you would like to book Dr. R. for speaking engagements, wellness workshops/retreats please contact her at: www.drremina.com

@DrRemina

Baghdad, Iraq
2004

www.ingramcontent.com/pod-product-compliance
Lightning Source LLC
Chambersburg PA
CBHW060419090426
42734CB00011B/2372